THE
SEVEN C'S
OF LEADERSHIP

Fulfilling Your God Given Call To
Inspire, Influence, and Serve

COACH MIKE JARVIS

with Chad Bonham

Coach Mike Jarvis and Chad Bonham would like to dedicate this book to their wives, Connie Jarvis and Amy Bonham, for their undying support and leadership within their individual households that has allowed their husbands to chase after their dreams and try to be all that God has called them to be.

ENDORSEMENTS

"During our time as head coaches in the New York metropolitan area, I witnessed firsthand how tough it was to play against a Mike Jarvis led team. His group was always together, prepared, and ready to battle. In *The Seven C's of Leadership*, Coach Jarvis lays out the essential ingredients of leadership. Every one of us has leadership within us, and this book offers fascinating principals that work in any setting—from the locker room to the executive board room."

–Jay Wright
NCAA Championship Men's Basketball Coach
Villanova University

"During my twenty-two years of service in our US Army, I learned that leadership comes down to Five C's – Courage, Competence, Commitment, Conviction, and Character. My belief is that if we had more people embracing those five fundamentals, our nation, our communities, the American society, would thrive. But, leave it up to renowned and accomplished college basketball coach, and my friend, Mike Jarvis, to expand upon what I learned into a superb, faith-based book on leadership, *The Seven C's of Leadership*. His book has already been accepted as the basis for a course at South Florida Bible College. Coach Jarvis, a man who knows a thing or two about leadership presents his seven C's (a Holy number)— Confidence, Courage, Character, Commitment, Communication, Community, Coach, and wraps it all up in Christ. As the song by Owl City says, 'In Christ alone, my hope is found. He is my Light, my Strength, my Song, this Cornerstone, this Solid Ground.' At a time in America when we are witnessing an epidemic of opioid addictions and deaths, along with suicides, we need Coach Jarvis' *Seven C's of Leadership*—grounded in the power of Christ alone where we should all make our stand. This is a must read for us all as we seek to be Christ centered leaders for our Constitutional Republic, these United States of America, and in our homes and communities."

–Lieutenant Colonel Allen B. West (U.S. Army, Retired)
Bronze Star Recipient
Member 112th U.S. Congress

"I love Mike Jarvis! The coach models his message. Read this book! *The Seven C's of Leadership* will elevate your leadership and help you bring out the best of the leaders around you."

–Tommy Kiedis
Senior Pastor
Spanish River Church, Boca Raton, Fla.

"It was in 2016 that I was first introduced to Coach Mike Jarvis after giving *Everybody Needs A Head Coach* to our Coaches at the NAIA Division II Men's Basketball National Championship FCA Coaches' Breakfast. We immediately developed a bond, and since then we have seen God use *Everybody Needs A Head Coach* to impact the lives of hundreds of coaches through the Coaches Bible Studies that I get to lead each week in South Central Missouri. His writing is open and honest, giving the reader the opportunity to relate to Coach Jarvis who has been given a high platform of influence and opportunity to work with some of the world's best coaches and athletes. That is why I am so excited about *The Seven C's of Leadership* as this book will help me continue to elevate the quality of coaches' Bible studies that I have been given the opportunity to do. Because of his books I am able to fully engage, equip, and empower our coaches to lead this culture of student athletes to be the best they can be physically, emotionally, and spiritually. I am honored to call Coach Mike Jarvis my friend, but most importantly my brother, in the Lord. It has been a pleasure to go down this road of ministry with him!"

–Brian Mitchell
South Central Missouri Area Director
Fellowship of Christian Athletes

"Dr. Coach Mike Jarvis (as I like to call him) is a role model that many need and can respect. His life-long career reflects integrity and outstanding character—the overlooked essentials needed (beyond talent) to be successful. *The Seven C's of Leadership* is a must-read for leaders, especially those in ministry. It provides invaluable insights on how to view leadership as the ability to influence others—an ability that everyone has. Every college should make this book required reading!"

–Dr. Mary Drabik
President, South Florida Bible College

"Mike Jarvis' new book, *The Seven C's of Leadership*, is a slam dunk and homerun all in one. He has always been an outstanding leader because he had the ability to decipher what true leadership really means. His leadership skills remind me of a quote from Booker T. Washington: 'The role of most leaders is to cause the people to think more of the leader. The role of the exceptional leader is to get the people to think more of themselves.' Mike was a master of making people think more of themselves. This is a must-read book because it is loaded with an arsenal of information on courage, confidence, commitment, and leadership, and will help you in a variety of ways, because the author wrote from his heart."

–Dale Brown
Head Men's Basketball Coach, LSU (1972-1997)
Member of the College Basketball Hall of Fame

"Why should people read this book? So they can awaken the leader and the leadership qualities that have been deposited within them. So they can show the world what it means to be Jesus Christ with skin on."

–Dr. Manny Ohonme
Founder, President and CEO, Samaritan's Feet International
Author of the best-selling book Sole Purpose

"Most people call him Coach. I call him Dad, and I feel like the luckiest and most blessed person in the world to have him as my father, my friend, my mentor, and my life coach. As I read *The Seven C's of Leadership*, I was able to relive so many unbelievable memories that we shared together. He was there when I took my first step. He was there to pick me up when I fell off my bike. He taught me how to throw a baseball and shoot a basketball. But most of all, he taught me about life, and that leadership begins in the home. At the age of three, I served as the bat boy for my dad's high school baseball team. I was the ball boy and stood by his side when his Cambridge Rindge and Latin High School teams won three consecutive state championships. At the age of 12, I served as his assistant coach at the McDonald's All American game and can honestly say that I coached Michael Jordan. In 1993, after graduating from Boston University, my dad and I made college basketball history when we became the first African American father/son coaching team in college basketball. Throughout my entire life, I have had the opportunity to watch, study, and learn from this confident, loving, and grateful servant of God. I hope and pray that *The Seven C's of Leadership* will help you and your family as much as it has helped me and mine.

–Mike Jarvis II
Director of Sports and Entertainment, The Hotaling Group

"The man affectionately known as, Mr. J., Coach J., Doc, Mr. Jarvis is still coaching alongside the Greatest Coach of all: Christ. The way that he has interwoven the gospel into this book is effortless and not preachy. I was instantly drawn in, because he was my high school basketball coach and my mentor, sharing things that I didn't know about him. The stories and references brought clarity and understanding to knowing the man that has guided so many of his players over the years. It was a breath of fresh air to see that through it all, you can't have the seven "C's" without Christ. I see this book being a teaching tool and a blessing to many."

–Ray Thomas
Broadcaster
Former Basketball Player at Cambridge Rindge and Latin High School

"I remember the day I got behind the wheel, and my dad told me to drive. Drive? Drive where? We were on the streets of Cambridge, and I knew that I was invincible and nothing was going to happen to me. Well, as I turned the corner, something connected with the car, and my confidence took a nosedive. I had my first fender bender, and at that moment, I felt like it was the end of the world. Thank goodness my dad, Coach Mike Jarvis, was with me in the car that day because if it had been someone else, perhaps I would have given up. He encouraged me to get back behind the wheel and drive us back home. The tears welled in my eyes the whole ride home, but I knew he wanted only the best for me. As I read *The Seven C's of Leadership*, it brought back so many memories and lessons that I learned from being the daughter of a coach, which I now apply to my life and that of my family. The biggest compliment I receive as a mother is that my children are respectful, confident, kind, courageous, and God-fearing young men. I wish I could take credit for these attributes, but I know that I cannot. Both of my parents taught me these things from a young age, and when I was ready to marry, I also found these traits in my spouse."

–Dana L. Shaiyen
Wife and Mother of Three Sons

"It gives me great honor to endorse Mike Jarvis' book, *The Seven C's of Leadership*. As in life, everything rises and falls on leadership. In the absence of quality leadership, people will follow anything or anyone. In a vacuum of leadership, Coach Jarvis is a breath of fresh air and encouragement. He is the consummate leader. Leaders lead! It's his DNA. If he's breathing, he's leading! Coach Jarvis is a championship coach on the hardwood floors of a basketball court, to the sandpit of a playground as an All-Pro Dad with his children who are now adults, and an All Star husband to his beautiful wife. Coach Mike Jarvis has been a leader all his life. Therefore, his incredible book is a fresh, cool drink from a deep well of wisdom and insight. This reminds me of another author, King Solomon, a man filled with wisdom and knowledge who made this statement in the book of Proverbs: 'The purpose in a man's heart is like deep water, but a man of understanding will draw it out.' (Proverbs 20:5, ESV). Coach Mike Jarvis lays out simple, yet profound eternal truths regarding Confidence, Courage, Character, Commitment, Communication, Community, and Christ. May I offer a word caution to the reader? The well is deep and the water cold, so instead of drinking, you might have to sip, as you dip, but it's worth the trip."

–Pastor Jeffery Singletary
Huddle Touch and Men of Valor

"I have known Mike Jarvis (Coach) for several years, 15 to be exact, as the principal and basketball coach at Calvert Catholic Schools. Calvert Catholic Schools have used Mike's first two books, *Skills for Life* and *Everyone Needs a Head Coach* as part of our enrichment program. Our students have found both books very informative, thought provoking, and very easy to read. I've been blessed to be a part of Mike's journey of enriching the lives of today's youth both practically as well as spiritually. His latest book, *The Seven C's of Leadership,* continues his on-going pursuit of inspiring, leading, and educating all people in all walks of life. I look forward to incorporating *The Seven C's of Leadership* into our curriculum. Calvert Catholic Schools has had the privilege of having him attend our Veterans Day programs as well as Face Time our seventh graders the last four years. This has been a blessing to have someone who is so giving of his time to interact with students so far away. *The Seven C's of Leadership* is a must-read, but more importantly, it's material needs to be put into practice. Coach has already blessed so many lives and will bless so many more with this book. I am honored and humbled to have him not only as a mentor, but more importantly as a friend in Christ."

–Ted Willman
Principal, Calvert Catholic Schools, Tiffin, Ohio

"In January of 2018, I asked Coach Jarvis to be the keynote speaker at the Leadership Prayer Breakfast for a non-profit organization, Take Stock in Children for Manatee County, Florida, where I serve as President and Chairman of the Board. Coach's speech centered on *The Seven C's of Leadership* and it was the first time that I heard him talk about it. As I listened, I recalled my days of being his manager for the Cambridge Rindge and Latin High School basketball team from 1981 to 1985. Upon reading the book, I realized what Coach Jarvis instilled in me through his mentorship over the years was *The Seven C's of Leadership.* The development of my personal life and my professional leadership style has been shaped as a result of these principles. As a longtime friend and mentor, I credit part of my personal growth and professional success to the relationship I have with Coach Jarvis. This book provides the basis of what we should strive for, so we can be the best person we can be, whether at work, home, on the court, or doing servant leadership. *The Seven C's of Leadership* are guiding principles for a life centered on leadership and servitude. I am blessed to have two head coaches: God and Coach Jarvis."

–Vincent P. Foderingham
Vice President, Risk Management, Feld Entertainment
President & Chairman of the Board of Directors, Take Stock in Children of Manatee County, Inc.
Basketball Team Manager, Cambridge Rindge & Latin High School, 1981-1985

"The Seven C's of Leadership is a must-read for every student athlete. In this book, Coach Jarvis does a masterful job of providing a roadmap to a successful life. Coach is a phenomenal individual who gives freely of himself and has now taken the time to bless us with his coaching insights. I highly recommend everyone in or outside of athletics to dive into this book and use it as a guide in your daily endeavors. In our Student ACES program, Coach Mike's *Seven C's of Leadership* has been a powerful and motivating tool for our captains, student athletes, and coaches. It has been tremendously successful in educating generations of student athletes and coaches, and I now look forward to utilizing these valuable concepts to develop the next generation of leaders. Coach Mike's deep faith in Christ the Savior is powerful and provides each of us the encouragement to lead our lives with character, honor, and integrity. A must-read!

–Buck Martinez
President and Co-Founder, Student ACES

"I read *The Seven C's of Leadership* twice, and I love it! Coach Jarvis has created something very special. I look forward to having all of eternity to spend with Jesus and classy folks like Mike Jarvis!"

–Dewey Clark
President, North Carolina Wesleyan College

"In *The Seven C's of Leadership*, Coach Jarvis does a phenomenal job of clearly articulating how all of us can be equipped as leaders, because God does not just call the highly equipped, but instead God equips everyone that is willing to acknowledge and embrace their own authentic calling in life."

-Darrin Gray
President, Center For Serving Leadership at Sagimore Institute
Principal Consultant, Brandirect, Inc.
Author, The Jersey Effect

"A man's greatest influences comes after he realizes he does not know it all and then starts a journey to know truth and make it known. Seldom do we see highly accomplished coaches like Coach Mike Jarvis start this journey after all the success he had in his 40-plus years of coaching college basketball. This book represents his journey and living out the truth he has discovered as a follower of Christ and lover of people. Since 2006, I have had the privilege of watching the transformation of Coach Jarvis. As a then 'retired' coach, and wondering what God had for him in life, we embarked on a basketball mission to Taiwan to discover coaching and competing in a different way. As I watched him serve with us, and coach our team to the gold medal in our international competition, I saw a man desiring to know and experience God and influence others for the gospel. As he writes about *The Seven C's of Leadership*, these are not just principles that have been experienced by Coach Jarvis, they have been discovered and lived out in very tangible ways as he uses his platform to influence others for good. His character and courage have been a cornerstone for his influence. Furthermore, his commitment to living out what God says is true about him, is adding value to leaders across the nation. In a world where leadership books abound, people are looking for the real stuff and someone that has experienced what they have written about. Coach has learned that to lead others well, he must follow well. This book is more about one man's journey to know and experience these principles and the impact they can have on others when lived out, than it is about the principles themselves. Coach Jarvis, the man I know now, would want nothing more than for your life to be transformed by living out these principles and leading you to influence others in a way God has intended. Enjoy the journey!"

-Eric Nelson
Executive Director of Sports TEAM/Basketball, Athletes in Action

PREFACE

Before you read *The Seven C's of Leadership*, there is an important foundation that needs to be established. Every time you read the word "truth," it is referring to a very specific concept commonly referred to as "Biblical Worldview." In order to set the tone for the rest of this book, here are seven key points to explain exactly what that means:

1. Absolute moral truths do exist, and they are clearly defined in the Bible:

"This is the verdict: Light has come into the world, but people loved darkness instead of light because their deeds were evil. Everyone who does evil hates the light, and will not come into the light for fear that their deeds will be exposed. But whoever lives by the truth comes into the light, so that it may be seen plainly that what they have done has been done in the sight of God." (John 3:19-21/NIV)

2. The Bible is accurate in *all* of its teachings:

"The entirety of Your word is truth, and all Your righteous judgments endure forever." (John 17:17/HCSB)

3. God created the universe and continues to rule it today. He is all powerful or omnipotent (Matthew 19:26), all knowing or omniscient (1 John 3:20), and everywhere or omnipresent (Psalm 139:7-12):

"Have you never heard? Have you never understood? The LORD is the everlasting God, the Creator of all the earth. He never grows weak or weary. No one can measure the depths of his understanding." (Isaiah 40:28/NLT)

4. Jesus Christ lived a sinless life during His ministry on earth:

"Therefore, since we have a great high priest who has ascended into heaven, Jesus the Son of God, let us hold firmly to the faith we profess. For we do not have a high priest who is unable to empathize with our weaknesses, but we have one who has been tempted in every

way, just as we are—yet he did not sin." (Hebrews 4:14-15/NIV)

5. Salvation through the blood that was shed by Jesus is a gift from God. Salvation is the only way to Heaven (John 14:6). It cannot be earned through good works or behavior, but rather by faith and in an act of repentance:

"This righteousness is given through faith in Jesus Christ to all who believe. There is no difference between Jew and Gentile, for all have sinned and fall short of the glory of God, and all are justified freely by his grace through the redemption that came by Christ Jesus. God presented Christ as a sacrifice of atonement, through the shedding of his blood—to be received by faith. He did this to demonstrate his righteousness, because in his forbearance he had left the sins committed beforehand unpunished—he did it to demonstrate his righteousness at the present time, so as to be just and the one who justifies those who have faith in Jesus." (Romans 3:22-26/NIV)

6. Satan (the Devil) is a real and present entity who seeks to separate man from God:

"Stay alert! Watch out for your great enemy, the devil. He prowls around like a roaring lion, looking for someone to devour." (1 Peter 5:8/NLT)

7. Christians have an obligation to share the Gospel (the Good News and the Bad News) with the unsaved.

"Therefore, go and make disciples of all the nations, baptizing them in the name of the Father and the Son and the Holy Spirit. Teach these new disciples to obey all the commands I have given you. And be sure of this: I am with you always, even to the end of the age." (Matthew 28:19-20/NLT)

FOREWORD
By Manny Ohonme

We live in a culture where people want to be heard; a culture that's obsessed with titles; a culture where it's about me, myself, and I; a culture where people want to get glory without really having to pay the price.

But being a kingdom-minded servant leader is counter to what the world says leadership is supposed to be. True leadership is about doing things that bring honor and glory to God. True leadership is about doing things that bring out the best in others. True leadership is about seeking meaningful recognition that will come one day when you stand before your King and hear those words, "Well done, my good and faithful servant."

I believe that the measure of a great leader is not found in their ability but in their availability—to be humble and to be ready to serve. I truly believe that's the greatest part of leaders.

In fact, God has designed us to be servant leaders. We are called to be an example and a model for the world to see. We do what we do so we can serve as a spotlight that points back to Christ. That's the essence of why we live and why we serve. We want to bring God glory in all that we do.

That belief is the reason we are launching a global leadership initiative through Samaritan's Feet. It's also why I'm so pleased that Coach Jarvis has written *The Seven C's of Leadership*.

Why should you read this book? So you can awaken the leader and the leadership qualities that have been deposited within you. So you can show the world what it means to be Jesus Christ with skin on.

I encourage you to dive deep into *The Seven C's of Leadership* and receive Coach Jarvis' vast knowledge and sagely wisdom. Take time to let the words jump off the page and into your heart as you strive to become the servant leader that God has called and equipped you to be.

–Manny Ohonme
Co-founder, CEO and President
Samaritan's Feet

INTRODUCTION

"If your actions inspire others to dream more and become more, you are a leader."
–John Quincy Adams
The Sixth President of the United States

There's a misconception about leadership that we as a society have believed for far too long, that great leaders are born with an abundance of talent, vision, and passion that makes it possible for them to inspire, influence, serve, and lead others. We often think that special abilities and privileged circumstances are required.

But if only a select few, people like Rev. Billy Graham, Jackie Robinson, Dr. Martin Luther King Jr., President John F. Kennedy, or Condoleezza Rice were chosen to be leaders based on their natural abilities or because they had formidable training and a desirable upbringing, you would be hard pressed to explain the phenomenon of my mother, Dorothy Irene Jarvis. She is a perfect example of how God does not call the equipped, but instead equips the called.

If it weren't for my mother, my personal journey as a leader and the writing of this book may not have ever occurred. She didn't come from wealth, did not attend college, and didn't seem to possess any out-of-the-ordinary aptitudes. She did, however, come from an environment of abounding love and was a humble servant of the Lord.

During her lifetime, my mom managed to do something quite extraordinary. She raised four children who went on to become good husbands and wives, loving parents, positive role models, well-respected members of the community, and productive American citizens. Those children also blessed her with 11 grandchildren and 20 great grandchildren.

How did she do it? She did it with the Lord's help and by applying distinct traits that I refer to as "The Seven C's of Leadership."

1. She had unshakeable Confidence in God. My mom knew whom she was and what she was called to do: be the best mother, friend, and person she could be. But most of all, she knew *whose* she was. She was a child of God. She knew she was never alone, and that

God was with her always. Her Confidence was in God's Word and the promise found in Jeremiah 29:11-13:

"For I know the plans I have for you," says the LORD. "They are plans for good and not for disaster, to give you a future and a hope. In those days when you pray, I will listen. If you look for me wholeheartedly, you will find me." (NLT)

2. She had the Courage to make the difficult decision to separate from my dad who had always struggled to keep his marriage vows and to provide for his family. She had the Courage to be a single mother and fight for every ounce of provision necessary to sustain her family while also looking after the needs of others. God supplied her with an incredible amount of Courage, because she knew that it was not her power that she had to depend on, but His promise to fulfill her needs.

3. She had impeccable Character. Every Sunday morning, no matter how tough the week had been or how tired she was, my mom made sure that we got up, got dressed, and went to church. She allowed God to help her develop strong inward Character that always showed up outwardly in those moments when adversity tried to keep her from doing what she knew was right. If I had to pick one word to describe my mother's Character, it would be "love." The apostle Paul must have been thinking about her when he wrote 1 Corinthians 13:4-8a:

"Love is patient, love is kind. It does not envy, it does not boast, it is not proud. It does not dishonor others, it is not self-seeking, it is not easily angered, it keeps no record of wrongs. Love does not delight in evil but rejoices with the truth. It always protects, always trusts, always hopes, always perseveres. Love never fails." (NIV)

Noted author and speaker, Jon Gordon, once said, "I learned from Mom that real leadership is about serving others by doing the little things with a big dose of selfless love."

4. She was a shining example of Commitment. This was perhaps one of my mom's greatest leadership attributes. There are too many examples to share and several are mentioned in my second book *Everybody Needs a Head Coach*.

But I'll never forget how mom visited Boston Children's Hospital every day for 11 months and stood outside waving to her little girl, my sister, Trudy, who was quarantined inside with scarlet fever. Or how she retired early from Polaroid to take care of her mother in Canada. How she managed those long, nine-hour drives back and forth, I'll never quite truly comprehend.

And of course, her Commitment to her children was unmatched. At one point, my mom was working two or three jobs and skipping meals to make sure she could meet all of our needs. I probably should have been working as well, but she afforded me the opportunity to go out and play ball and pursue my athletic dreams.

5. She understood the importance of Communication. She lovingly and, when necessary, forcefully let us know our responsibilities in the household. My mom made sure we understood that we would have to work as a team if we were going to survive—like the time she gave me my one and only whooping for claiming it wasn't my job to look out for my brother who had gone fishing and was an hour late for dinner. Mom knew that listening was also an important part of Communication. She always asked great questions, because she mastered the art of listening.

6. She valued the idea of Community. Mom was always ready to lend a helping hand to the less fortunate or those in need. The Meals on Wheels program was near and dear to her heart. On more than one occasion, I was invited to go with my mom to deliver the meals that she had prepared. I can't describe how happy the people were to see her and how good that made her feel. She truly was a faithful servant not only to her family and her church, but also to many others within her small but significant circle of influence.

7. She was my first Coach—not literally on the ball field or on the court, but in life. She showed me the importance of hard work and taught me to finish what you start. My mom taught me that life is a team game and how important it is to surround yourself with people that you can rely on for guidance, discipline, and support. Most importantly, my mom mentored me in those pivotal moments throughout my formidable years.

Above all else, everything she did was a reflection of Christ. I can't tell you how many times I saw her on her hands and knees, praying at her bedside. She didn't pray for a new car or a new house or for money. She prayed to the good Lord for her kids. It was her desire that she live like Christ, and for Christ, and that her children would also grow up in the fear (respect) of the Lord. She wanted her family to know and understand the value of having a relationship with Him.

Mom was 98 years and seven months old when she passed away. In fact, she went to be with the Lord during the writing of this book. So it only seemed appropriate that she receive due credit for teaching me what I now call *The Seven C's of Leadership*. That's why this book is more than just a cleverly titled self-help book. I can't take credit for the concept. No, it was my dear mother who first exemplified those seven attributes in my life and was my first glimpse of the most important C of them all—Christ.

As you read this book, there are three important things I hope you learn:

1. Everybody is a leader. That means *everybody*—the preschool child on the playground, the janitor who works tirelessly up and down the hallways of a corporate high-rise, the single mom working two jobs, the CEO of a Fortune 500 company, the elected government official, and the superstar athlete or coach to whom God has presented an incredible platform. At some point in your life, you will have an opportunity to lead somebody else, and you'll need to be ready when that time comes if it hasn't already presented itself.

"You are the light of the world. A town built on a hill cannot be hidden. Neither do people light a lamp and put it under a bowl. Instead they put it on its stand, and it gives light to everyone in the house. In the same way, let your light shine before others, that they may see your good deeds and glorify your Father in heaven." (Matthew 5:13-16/NIV)

2. Everybody is called to be a leader. It's one thing to understand that you have leadership capabilities built into your

DNA. But it is incredibly empowering when you realize that leadership is part of a divine plan for your life. You are here for a purpose, and part of that purpose is to be a leader to those people that God has placed within your circle of influence. It doesn't matter if that circle holds one person or thousands of people. You have the ability to influence people in the service of God.

"Brothers and sisters, think of what you were when you were called. Not many of you were wise by human standards; not many were influential; not many were of noble birth. But God chose the foolish things of the world to shame the wise; God chose the weak things of the world to shame the strong. God chose the lowly things of this world and the despised things—and the things that are not—to nullify the things that are, so that no one may boast before him." (1 Corinthians 1:26-29/NIV)

3. Everybody needs to follow THE Leader. Just like everything else in life, leadership is a pointless and empty proposition if exercised apart from a relationship with Jesus Christ. And when it comes to learning about leadership, there's no better example than the way Jesus led His disciples—strong, decisive, wise, and in the countercultural form of a servant.

"Jesus called them together and said, 'You know that the rulers of the Gentiles lord it over them, and their high officials exercise authority over them. Not so with you. Instead, whoever wants to become great among you must be your servant, and whoever wants to be first must be your slave—just as the Son of Man did not come to be served, but to serve, and to give his life as a ransom for many.'" (Matthew 20:25-28/NIV)

For the next 12 chapters, we will take a closer look at these vital principles. Some of them (such as Character, Communication, Community, and Coach) will be discussed over the course of two or three chapters so we can make sure to take a close look at their inward and outward expressions. After we conclude the book with a look at Christ (the most important C), we will also share a bonus chapter on another vital C (Cash) that is sometimes overlooked and discover what it looks like to be biblical stewards of our finances and resources.

At the end of each chapter, there are study questions that you can answer on your own or in a group setting. And finally, to help you apply these principles to your life, each chapter also includes a section at the end with some ways that you can "Follow Through" on your desire to improve your leadership skills. You don't have to do everything listed, but we highly recommend that you try to do at least one thing per chapter. It will be well worth the effort—we promise!

Thanks so much for sharing some of your time and allowing us into your life. We look forward to you joining us on this journey as we unpack *The Seven C's of Leadership*.

–Coach Mike Jarvis

TABLE OF CONTENTS

CHAPTER ONE: CONFIDENCE
KNOWING WHO YOU ARE

"Being confident of this, that he who began a good work in you will carry it on to completion until the day of Christ Jesus."
–Philippians 1:6 (NIV)

There's no question that my mom deserves so much of the credit for helping me become a more effective leader as a husband, father, coach, and active member of my church and community, and it all started with the confidence she instilled in me from a very young age.

But there were a few other people, including my older brother, Richard, and my sister, Trudy, that built on that foundation and helped me develop confidence in some specific areas of my life.

COACHING THE COACH

Take for instance my first coach, "Stretch" Headley, who coached the neighborhood Little League team.

It was April 11, 1956, when I first met Stretch. I was walking across the neighborhood baseball field on the way to the basketball court to shoot some hoops with the ball that my brother, Richard, had just given me for my birthday. I heard someone calling me.

"Crisco! Crisco! C'mon over here!"

Back then everybody had a nickname. Mine was "Crisco." It was a nice way for my friends to call me fatso without hurting my feelings.

The voice belonged to Stretch, so I tucked the basketball under my right arm and ran over to the baseball diamond as fast as I could. When I arrived, Stretch asked me if I wanted to play for his team. That was an easy question to answer. Of course I did. I jumped at the opportunity to play on my first organized team along with my buddies.

What I didn't realize at the time was Stretch only had eight players and needed a ninth kid to complete the team. All the positions were filled except one. Stretch needed a catcher. On most Little League teams back then, the chubby kid usually filled that position. I not only accepted the role, but I loved it.

19

As I look back upon that day, I now know that it was the beginning of my coaching career. Thanks to Stretch, I became the coach on the field and the leader on the team.

Before long, I was telling the other players what to do. I told the pitcher what pitch to throw, the third baseman to move in, and the outfielders to move over. I could call a timeout anytime I wanted to hold a meeting with the pitcher and the infielders at the pitcher's mound. Sometimes I told the players what to do just because I could.

God put Stretch in my life at a very critical time, and his name was prophetic because he helped me expand my horizons, helped me grow, and helped me stretch my physical and intellectual muscles. He made me do things I wouldn't have done on my own. Stretch was tough, but he coached and disciplined me in a loving way.

Most importantly, Stretch gave me the Confidence to lead my teammates and myself.

Several years later, I earned a spot on the men's basketball team at Northeastern University in Boston, Massachusetts. Eventually I was awarded a half scholarship. This was a big deal because at the time (early '60s) there were only a handful of black players, and no black head coaches, in New England.

My coach was the legendary Dick Dukeshire who led that program for thirteen years before moving on to become the Greek national coach. I didn't appreciate his genius as a teacher and coach, because I spent most of my time complaining about my lack of playing time.

During my sophomore year, I quit the team and returned home to work as a short order cook at my brother's fish and chips store across the street from my house in Cambridge. As I grew tired of getting burned, and realized how much I missed the game and my teammates, I took Richard's advice, ate some humble pie, and begged Coach Dukeshire to allow me to rejoin the team. Thankfully, he accepted my apology and was gracious enough to give me a second chance.

When I returned to the team the following year, my attitude and focus changed dramatically. I didn't play a lot more, but during my time on the bench, I decided that I wanted to return to my high school to teach Physical Education and coach the boys' basketball team. I was going to teach the fundamentals of basketball and life.

Before going to bed every night, I would pull out my blue, three-hole notebook and write down all of the plays and teaching points I had learned that day in practice. Throughout my coaching career I would refer to this as my Coaching Bible.

Equally important was the fact that Coach Dukeshire named me captain of the third team. My teammates gave me the nickname "Captain Darby" after actor James Garner's role in a popular 1958 movie about a real life Army platoon called *Darby's Rangers*.

After all the grief I put my coach and teammates through, they still saw my potential as a leader—even when I didn't see it in myself. My role was to get my third string teammates to play inspired defense, and prepare the top players for battle. I accepted and fully embraced that role, and our team was better than ever. Captain Darby and his Rangers took pride in the success of the improvement of our star athletes, which included two future NBA players, Rick Weitzman (Boston Celtics) and Harry Barnes (San Diego Clippers).

Whenever there was an issue or a problem, the team would come to me, express their concerns, and ask me to talk to the coach on the team's behalf. As the liaison between the players and the coach, I started interacting with him in a leadership position. That's when I realized that you don't have to be the coach, the star player, or the captain to be a leader. You can be a leader even if you're the last man on the team, a Little League catcher named "Crisco," or a third string point guard named "Captain Darby."

I didn't realize it until much later, but both of these men (Stretch and Coach Dukeshire) were coaching the future coach that I had yet to become. And it all started with the confidence they gave me—the Confidence required to lead.

THE KEY TO CONFIDENCE

In between my first coach and my last coach, God placed another important person in my life. That person was Ms. Regina B. Key, my eighth grade teacher at Houghton Grammar School in Cambridge.

Ms. Key was not only a great teacher, but she was a great leader who truly loved her students and the Lord. Every morning, our day would begin as we stood and pledged our allegiance to the United States flag and said The Lord's Prayer. She gave us what we needed, not what we wanted, and she wasn't concerned about being politically correct.

Ms. Key nominated me for my first non-athletic award—the John F. Burke Citizenship Award—given to the eighth grade boy and girl that displayed the best character and sportsmanship.

Perhaps most importantly, Ms. Key gave me the Confidence to speak in public—a skill that has been with me throughout my adult life as a teacher, coach, and motivational speaker. She selected me to deliver the keynote speech at our eighth grade graduation. The speech was named "All Aboard For Space," and I spoke about America's space race against the Russians. I practiced that speech for weeks with my sister, Trudy. I looked into her eyes and her smiling face the entire graduation speech. It was one of those days I will never forget.

I didn't see myself as a leader, but Ms. Key did. That's what leaders do. They help others see who they can become and where they are going, and then they give them the tools to get there. They help others do things that they wouldn't normally do. They push them, stretch them, and help them fulfill their God-ordained purpose.

Because of Ms. Key's faith in God and the Confidence she had in me, I was well prepared for the transition from grammar school to high school and beyond.

DIVINE PROVIDENCE

Confidence. It's something that we all strive to obtain, but something that's not easy to get and even more difficult to keep. That's because Confidence is often based on what we do or what others do. When we make mistakes or when others let us down, it can shake our Confidence or our belief in ourselves. We live in an imperfect world where no one is completely shielded from negative circumstances. When bad things happen or when things don't go as we planned, our Confidence can take a significant hit, and we can be easily knocked off our feet.

In the Old Testament, a young man named Joseph displays great Confidence despite dealing with some incredible adversity. He is able to do so because of something called providence. According to dictionary.com, some common definitions of providence include, "the foreseeing care and guidance of God," "a manifestation of divine care or direction," and "timely preparation for future eventualities." Joseph truly understood this concept. He knew that God had a purpose for everything, good or bad, and that He would always provide.

Joseph's Confidence was rooted in his understanding of who he was. He was Jacob's favorite son, because he was born to him in his old age. One day, Jacob gave Joseph a special gift: a beautiful robe (Genesis 37:3-4). Joseph's brothers hated him because of their father's partiality. They couldn't say a kind word to him.

On two occasions, Joseph had dreams that he shared with his brothers. In one of those dreams, the sun, the moon, and eleven stars (a representation of his father, mother, and brothers) all bowed to him. His brothers became so enraged that they plotted to kill him and later revised that plan to fake his death and sell him into slavery (Genesis 37:12-34). This set Joseph's life on a path that was unexpectedly difficult. These dreams were God's way of showing Joseph that He would providentially guide his steps—even when the road was rough.

In Egypt, Joseph's story took many twists and turns. After gaining favor with his master, he was put in prison after his master's wife falsely accused Joseph of attempted rape. But while incarcerated, the warden put Joseph in charge of the entire prisoner population (Genesis 39). During his time in prison he became known for interpreting dreams.

After two years in prison, Joseph was called to appear before Pharaoh and explain to him a troubling vision of his own. God revealed to Joseph that Egypt was going to have seven years of plentiful harvest followed by seven years of famine. Pharaoh then chose Joseph to administer a relief program to meet the challenge (Genesis 41:1-41).

This led to a powerful meeting between Joseph and his brothers, who came to Egypt seeking food during the famine (Genesis 42-45). Because Joseph understood providence, he had the Confidence to stand before his brothers and not only help them, but forgive them as well.

"You intended to harm me, but God intended it all for good. He brought me to this position so I could save the lives of many people." (Genesis 50:20/NLT)

DIVINE PURPOSE

Purpose. It's a little word that has a big meaning. And like providence, it plays a direct role in our ability to obtain Confidence. Simply put, purpose is the reason why someone or something exists, or the reason that we do the things we do.

When it comes to Confidence, the concept of purpose is everything. If you don't know why you're here, and you don't know why you do the things you do, it's impossible to have a solid foundation of Confidence to stand upon.

Jesus showed uncommon Confidence throughout his life and ministry on the earth, but it was first documented within a unique story that took place when He was a boy:

"Every year Jesus' parents went to Jerusalem for the Festival of the Passover. When he was twelve years old, they went up to the festival, according to the custom. After the festival was over, while his parents were returning home, the boy Jesus stayed behind in Jerusalem, but they were unaware of it. Thinking he was in their company, they traveled on for a day. Then they began looking for him among their relatives and friends. When they did not find him, they went back to Jerusalem to look for him. After three days, they found him in the temple courts, sitting among the teachers, listening to them, and asking them questions. Everyone who heard him was amazed at his understanding and his answers. When his parents saw him, they were astonished. His mother said to him, 'Son, why have you treated us like this? Your father and I have been anxiously searching for you.' 'Why were you searching for me?' he asked. 'Didn't you know I had to be in my Father's house?' But they did not understand what he was saying to them. Then he went down to Nazareth with them and was obedient to them. But his mother treasured all these things in her heart. And Jesus grew in wisdom and stature, and in favor with God and man." (Luke 2:41-52)

Even as a boy, Jesus understood that He had a divine purpose. Because of that, He was able to sit confidently before the Jewish teachers and conduct meaningful conversation about deep, spiritual matters. Jesus wasn't afraid to be away from His parents. He was too entrenched in His greater purpose to be bogged down with the typical cares or distractions that a pre-teen might encounter.

The same is true for us today. When we understand that we belong to God and are under his care (like Joseph), and when we understand that we have a definitive purpose for being on this earth (like Jesus), then we can have an unshakable Confidence in everything we do, no matter the circumstances around us and no matter what other people may think, say, or do.

SEVEN KEYS TO CONFIDENCE

Confidence is a life skill that can be learned, practiced, and mastered. And just like any other skill, once you master it, everything else in your life can change. At the same time, true Confidence only comes from understanding who we are in Christ and what we have been called to do with our lives. Here are seven principles that can help you lay a solid foundation of Confidence:

1. Know Who You Are. You are a child of God, created in His image (Genesis 1:27). There's no greater Confidence builder than understanding that powerful truth.

"I knew you before I formed you in your mother's womb. Before you were born, I set you apart and appointed you as my prophet to the nations." (Jeremiah 1:5/NLT)

2. Know Whose You Are. Being a child of God means you belong to God—not as His property, but as His valued creation. But you have to accept His Son, Jesus Christ (1 John 1:9), and submit to His authority (Matthew 28:18) if you want to lay claim to the full Confidence that comes with that divine relationship.

"So in Christ Jesus you are all children of God through faith." (Galatians 3:26/NIV)

3. Know The Truth. God's Word must be the foundation for everything you do. Confidence is only sustainable when it is rooted and grounded in His unshakeable truth.

"The Word became flesh and made his dwelling among us. We have seen His glory, the glory of the one and only Son, who came from the Father, full of grace and truth." (John 1:14/NIV)

4. Know Where You Are Going. You have a God-given purpose (Jeremiah 29:11), and that purpose drives your goals. If you know where you're going (and it's in the direction that God has laid out for you), you can walk confidently, knowing that everything is going to be okay even when things are not going as planned.

"Commit to the LORD whatever you do, and he will establish your plans." (Proverbs 16:3/NIV)

5. Know Your Strengths. You have definable gifts and talents. Play to them. Work to make them even stronger. There's a reason you have those strengths, and God wants to use them for His purposes.

"For just as each of us has one body with many members, and these members do not all have the same function, so in Christ we, though many, form one body, and each member belongs to all the others. We have different gifts, according to the grace given to each of us. If your gift is prophesying, then prophesy in accordance with your faith; if it is serving, then serve; if it is teaching, then teach; if it is to encourage, then give encouragement; if it is giving, then give generously; if it is to lead, do it diligently; if it is to show mercy, do it cheerfully." (Romans 12:4-8/NIV)

6. Know Your Weaknesses. Have a sober self-assessment of who you are (Romans 12:3) and where you fall short. Acknowledge those areas of your life that are holding you back, so you can improve on your weaknesses and dive deeper into the Confidence of God.

"He gives power to the weak and strength to the powerless." (Isaiah 40:29/NLT)

7. Know Your Source. All of your talents and abilities come from God. If you try to claim them as your own, your Confidence will be sitting on shaky ground, and will not be able to withstand the adversity that you will face on a daily basis.

"Every good and perfect gift is from above, coming down from the Father of the heavenly lights, who does not change like shifting shadows." (James 1:17/NIV)

STUDY QUESTIONS

1. How do you define the word "Confidence?"

2. What are some things in which you are Confident? What are some things in which you lack Confidence? Explain.

3. Who are some people throughout your life that have built up your Confidence?

4. How often do you think about who you are and whose you are?

5. What does the word "providence" mean to you? Can you describe a time when you felt like God was directing your path?

6. Do you feel like you have a divine purpose? Explain.

7. What are some things you can start doing today that will help you have more Confidence in who you are, whose you are, and what you are called to do?

FOLLOW THROUGH

• Find a Confidence "buddy" or partner—someone who boosts your Confidence—and call them at least once a week for a pep talk.

• Find a song that strengthens your Confidence and listen to it when needed.

• Practice smiling throughout the day. Every time you smile, your brain throws a feel-good party!

• Read through and meditate on the scriptures found throughout this chapter. If you'd like to do some additional Bible study on Confidence, here are some verses to get you started: Jeremiah 1:5, Proverbs 16:3, Philippians 1:6.

PRAYER

Lord, help me to fully understand who I am in Christ and to fully embrace whose I am. Continue to show me Truth so that I might have divine Confidence in my strengths, and so that I might surrender my weaknesses to You. I want to fulfill Your purpose for my life and become the person that You have called me to be. Amen.

CHAPTER TWO: COURAGE
STANDING FOR TRUTH

"Have I not commanded you? Be strong and courageous. Do not be afraid; do not be discouraged, for the LORD your God will be with you wherever you go."
–Joshua 1:9 (NIV)

If Confidence is the foundation, then the first step into bold, active leadership is Courage. You must have Courage to make tough decisions. You must have Courage to fight through adversity. You must have Courage to stand up for what's right. You must have Courage if you're going to move forward in God's calling on your life.

So what exactly is Courage?

Courage is going against the grain. Courage is refusing to lead based on popular opinions. Courage is going against the opposition. Courage is forging ahead when more people disagree than agree. Courage is stepping out on the ledge. Courage is not being afraid to fail, and getting back up again when you do fail.

Here's another important question: Where does Courage come from?

People with courage know that what they are doing is right, but understanding what's right must be grounded in the truth of God's Word. As we talked about in chapter one, truth is the foundation of Confidence, and it's also the only way anyone can truly be bold and courageous. That's the kind of leader people are looking to follow. That's the kind of leader people will trust to take them down the right path.

A KID NAMED MOSES

In 1986, I accepted my first college head coaching job at Boston University and quickly hit the recruiting trail. My assistant coach, Ed Meyers, received a call from his friend, Rubin Fuller, who was the Athletic Director and boys' basketball coach at Mt. Pleasant High School in South Carolina. Coach Fuller had a kid he wanted us to consider as a possible addition to the program. His name was Ronnie Moses.

Based on Ed's evaluation and Coach Fuller's high praise, I decided to travel to South Carolina and meet Ronnie. I was prepared to offer him a scholarship, but first I wanted to get to know the person, not just the athlete.

When I drove up to the school, I saw a one-story building that looked like a large trailer home. The total enrollment at the high school was 300. Ronnie's graduating class was 75 students. Everyone on the campus was African American, and most of the kids were from low-income homes. Many of them were also the products of single-parent families that had lost their dads to the Vietnam War. Ronnie had an equally difficult childhood. His mother died when he was 11 years old and from that point his older brother and his sister-in-law raised him.

In many ways, Ronnie's school reminded me of the Houghton Grammar School that I attended back in Cambridge. The teachers loved their students and taught them the basics. Most importantly, they were godly men and women who believed in the kids and their futures.

I'll never forget the first time I saw Ronnie as he walked across the football field to meet with me. He stood 6 feet 7 inches tall and weighed 230 pounds. He looked more like a tackle than a power forward, but he was soft spoken, looked me right in the eye, and said "yes sir" and "no sir" every time he replied. Ronnie was very humble and immediately accepted my scholarship offer. All he needed to know was when he needed to report to school.

A few months later, Ronnie flew on a plane for the first time. When his flight arrived at Boston's Logan Airport, I was there to meet him at the gate. We greeted each other with a smile and a firm handshake before proceeding to baggage claim. We stood there as the other passengers grabbed their luggage and left, but Ronnie's bags never arrived.

"Well son, it looks like we need to go to the office and file a lost baggage claim," I told Ronnie.

"But Coach," he replied. "This is all I've got."

To my surprise, Ronnie's entire belongings were stuffed into a duffle bag that he had been carrying over his shoulder. He came to Boston University with a pair of shoes, a pair of slacks, some underwear, a shaving kit, and the clothes on his back. Ronnie had more clothes back home, but coming from the warm climate in South

Carolina, he wasn't prepared for the harsh winters he would endure in Boston.

Maybe he's going to buy a new cold weather wardrobe here, I thought to myself. So I asked him what he needed while estimating how much he would need to pay.

"How much money did you bring?" I asked.

That's when Ronnie told me that Coach Fuller had given him some cash to help him out for the year. I almost fell to the floor when he told me that $22 was all he had in his pocket. Needless to say, we found a way to help Ronnie get what he needed. Our coaching staff worked with Reverend Robert Thornberg, the university chaplain at Marsh Chapel, to provide Ronnie with some donated clothes.

But now I had an even bigger question on my mind.

"Ronnie," I asked as we drove to the campus. "What made you decide to take a leap of faith and come to Boston University?"

I'll never forget his response.

"Coach, my hero was Dr. Martin Luther King," he said. "And if Boston University was good enough for him, it's good enough for me."

It was quite the culture shock as Ronnie came from an entirely black school in a small southern town and was now at a predominately white university in one of the biggest and most expensive cities in the country. But he developed a great relationship with his Irish Catholic roommate, Jeff Timberlake, and garnered incredible support, encouragement, and love from his academic advisor, Karen Ercole. Ronnie worked hard and thrived in the loving family environment we had created.

Many years later, Ronnie explained to me how three other "C's" made all the difference. It started with my wife, Connie. She showed him compassion by inviting him into our home and cooking for him on a regular basis. Ronnie especially enjoyed spending time with us every Sunday for dinner. He really loved Connie's macaroni and cheese. In fact, he was at our house so often, the other players teased him with the nickname "Ronnie Jarvis."

He usually left our home on Sundays about five to seven pounds heavier, and the next afternoon at practice, I always had to work him extra hard to get him back into shape. But Ronnie didn't mind. Being a part of our family gave him the courage to stay in Boston and become the leader he had been called to be.

On the court, he had a successful career that culminated in an exceptional senior season. That year, Ronnie was our second leading scorer and our leading rebounder. He helped lead the team to an American East Conference championship and a berth in the NCAA Tournament.

Most importantly, he left Boston University with a Sociology Degree and later earned his Master's Degree in Information Technology with an emphasis in Network Security. He now lives in St. Robert, Missouri, with his wife of 25 years, Chylon, and his two daughters, where he owns and manages real estate.

But those accomplishments aren't what I'll remember about Ronnie Moses. Anytime I hear his name, the word Courage comes to mind. It could have been his first, middle, or last name. It took Courage to get on that plane and leave South Carolina. It took Courage to become the first person in his family to graduate from college. It took Courage to step out of his comfort zone to become a leader on the court, in the classroom, and now in his family and in his community.

TWO KENNEDYS AND A KING

Historically, bold and courageous leaders trying to do the right thing often have a target on their backs. We've seen many instances right here in the United States of America. Abraham Lincoln is one of our nation's most tragic examples. On April 15, 1865, John Wilkes Booth assassinated Lincoln just five days after General Robert E. Lee and the Confederate Army of Northern Virginia surrendered, and less than a month before the official end of the Civil War, which ended slavery.

Lincoln is one of many great examples of courageous leadership. In my lifetime, there were three other courageous leaders who impacted me deeply. All three of them were pictures of Courage amid the volatile Civil Rights Movement in the 1960s.

First, there was President John F. Kennedy who made great strides in bringing people together. Not only was he a proponent of the Civil Rights Act of 1964 (which passed eight months after his death), President Kennedy was also a World War II hero, and as President, boldly proclaimed that the United States would be the first to send a man to the moon.

Second, there was his younger brother, Robert F. Kennedy, who served as the U.S. Attorney General and was likely to become a Presidential nominee prior to his untimely death in 1968. Like his brother, Attorney General Kennedy was a World War II veteran. He was also a civil rights advocate and passionate voice for the poor.

The third man was Dr. Martin Luther King. He was someone I shared in common with Ronnie Moses. Dr. King was a hero to both of us. In September of 1963, he famously gave his "I Have A Dream" speech at the National Mall in Washington D.C. A year and a half later, I marched in Boston's biggest freedom march with thousands from the surrounding communities. I remember walking down Columbus Avenue while holding my future wife, Connie's, hand on my right and the hand of an elderly white man on my left.

Dr. King united poor people. He united people of all colors. He fought for justice, for the good of the country, and as he stated in his "I Have A Dream" speech, that "All men, black and white, should be guaranteed their unalienable rights of life, liberty, and the pursuit of happiness."

But as history sadly reminds us, all three of these men (like Lincoln) were assassinated before they could see the fulfillment of their dreams. They must have known that they were putting their lives on the line, yet they still had the Courage to do what they believed was right even when that meant putting themselves in harm's way.

Perhaps that fact was most evident in Dr. King's prophetic "Mountaintop" speech that was given at the Mason Temple in Memphis, Tennessee on April 3, 1968—one day before he was shot and killed:

"Well, I don't know what will happen now. We've got some difficult days ahead. But it really doesn't matter with me now, because I've been to the mountaintop. And I don't mind. Like anybody, I would like to live a long life—longevity has its place. But I'm not concerned about that now. I just want to do God's will. And He's allowed me to go up to the mountain. And I've looked over, and I've seen the Promised Land. I may not get there with you. But I want you to know tonight, that we, as a people, will get to the promised land. So I'm happy, tonight. I'm not worried about anything, I'm not fearing any man. Mine eyes have seen the glory of the coming of the Lord."

QUIET COURAGE

But what if you don't feel like you are in a position of power or authority? What if you don't come from an influential family, or you don't have a big platform? What if you don't have the ability to capture people's attention with a speech? And what if being courageous doesn't seem like it will make much of a difference? Maybe my dear mother felt that way. After all, no one was watching her courageously lead her children and teaching them right from wrong.

There might be no better historical example of that same kind of quiet Courage than a little lady named Rosa Parks. Not many people outside of her community in Montgomery, Alabama, knew her name before December 1, 1955. But now, she is one of the most recognized figures in American history.

Why is that? Why would this 42-year old woman become a household name? It happened because of one simple, but profound action. Instead of giving up her place in the colored section of the bus for a white passenger (after the white section had filled up), Rosa Parks had the courage to stand her ground. Her bold decision helped change things for the better.

GOD'S COURAGEOUS WARRIOR

Earlier, you read the story about a basketball player named Ronnie Moses who courageously left South Carolina to play for my team at Boston University. His biblical namesake also had a lot of Courage as he led the Israelites out of Egyptian slavery. That Moses, however, eventually had to give up his leadership to a young man named Joshua.

The Bible doesn't tell us much about Joshua other than the fact that he was born in Egypt prior to the Exodus, his father was Nun, and he was from the tribe of Ephraim. In other words, Joshua wasn't someone of great renown or influential heritage. Yet God raised him up to first serve as Moses' assistant and to ultimately become the leader of the Israelites.

Even before Joshua took over, he showed incredible Courage as one of the twelve spies charged with scouting Canaan, the land that God promised to give His people. Joshua and Caleb were the only two men who brought back a good report while the other ten cowered in fear because of the giants that lived there (Numbers 13:1-33).

Joshua is most famous for leading the Israelites in the Battle of Jericho (Joshua 6). He faithfully followed God's unconventional instructions. The army walked around the walls of the city one time for six days each and then seven times on the seventh day. Each day, the priests blew their horns during the march. Then, at the end of the seventh day, the priests blew their horns one last time and the armies gave a loud shout. The Walls of Jericho came tumbling down, and the city was overtaken.

Why was Joshua so confident? Perhaps it was because he had seen God perform miracle after miracle to help the Israelites escape Egypt. Or maybe it was because he had learned directly from a courageous man like Moses. I have a feeling, however, that it was the direct Communication from God that emboldened Joshua to lead with Confidence and strength.

Have I not commanded you? Be strong and courageous. Do not be afraid; do not be discouraged, for the LORD your God will be with you wherever you go." (Joshua 1:9/NIV)

God was with Joshua, and Joshua had faith in God's plan. That faith gave him the Confidence to do what God told him to do. His Confidence in God's power gave him the Courage to boldly lead the Israelites into its destiny.

THE TEMPLE, THE GARDEN, AND THE CROSS

In chapter one, we talked about the Confidence that Jesus had because of His relationship with God. That Confidence was the foundation for those times when He displayed courageous leadership. Although Jesus was known for His humble and meek spirit, there were times when His passion for righteousness required bold action.

Such was the case when He vigorously chased the merchants and moneychangers out of the Temple in Jerusalem during Passover.

"Making a whip of cords, he drove all of them out of the temple, both the sheep and the cattle. He also poured out the coins of the moneychangers and overturned their tables. He told those who were selling the doves, 'Take these things out of here! Stop making my Father's house a marketplace!" (John 2:15-16/NRSV)

Jesus knew this would anger the Jewish leaders. He knew His actions would put a target on His back. It didn't matter, because He also knew what He was called to do, and fear was not going to keep Him from working out God's plan.

This held even truer during the days leading up to His death. Jesus knew what was about to happen on Calvary. He clearly understood that He would be arrested, unjustly tried, brutally tortured, and then crucified on a criminal's cross (as described in Matthew 27). Still, while praying in the Garden of Gethsemane, Jesus courageously accepted His God-ordained fate.

"Father, if you are willing, take this cup from me; yet not my will, but yours be done." (Luke 22:42/NIV)

It was on that cross where Jesus put the ultimate act of Courage on full display. And the only reason He was able to endure the pain and the rejection and the shame was because He saw the big picture. Jesus knew why He needed to die. Jesus understood that this was the only way man could ever be reconciled with God. That truth didn't make it easy, but it did give Him the Courage to go through with the plan, even though He could have walked away before His arrest.

Jesus knew His Father's plan and trusted the plan. His belief in the plan and His great love for all people gave Him the Courage to follow through with that plan even unto death. That's the kind of Courage that all leaders should aspire to display—Courage that is rooted in a Confidence that only comes from knowing truth.

SEVEN KEYS TO COURAGE (OR STANDING FOR TRUTH)

In this chapter, we've talked about a few examples of bold, courageous leadership. And while the circumstances behind each story were different, there was one common denominator that allowed these people to stand strong—they all had that Confidence in their purpose (as discussed in chapter one) and understood what was at stake. Here are seven biblical keys to help you follow in their footsteps as another bold, courageous leader willing to step out and fulfill God's call for your life:

1. Get Your Marching Orders. Listen for the Leader's instruction. This happens through prayer, through the reading of

God's Word, and being sensitive to the Holy Spirit in your life. Know what you are called to do and then prepare to do it.

"Keep this Book of the Law always on your lips; meditate on it day and night, so that you may be careful to do everything written in it. Then you will be prosperous and successful." (Joshua 1:8/NIV)

2. Define The Mission. Make a plan and write it down. Set goals that you reach along the way as you live out the purpose to which you've been called.

"The plans of the diligent lead to profit as surely as haste leads to poverty." (Proverbs 21:5/NIV)

3. Stay The Course. Stick to the plan. Don't waver from it. God put that plan into place for a purpose and He knows best—even when things don't seem to make sense.

"Give careful thought to the paths for your feet
and be steadfast in all your ways.
Do not turn to the right or the left;
keep your foot from evil." (Proverbs 4:26-27/NIV)

4. Stand Firm. Sometimes God's plan will look silly, and others will question what you are doing. But just like Joshua, don't waver, and press through your fear and doubt so you can block out the naysayers that try to stop you.

"Be on your guard; stand firm in the faith; be courageous; be strong." (1 Corinthians 16:13/NIV)

5. Be Prepared For Adversity. Bad things are going to happen, so be ready. And when adversity comes, don't let it shake you up, slow you down, or push you off the path, but rather be encouraged that all adversity is meant for your good.

"Consider it pure joy, my brothers and sisters, whenever you face trials of many kinds, because you know that the testing of your faith produces perseverance." (James 1:2-3/NIV)

6. Adjust And Adapt. All leaders make mistakes. When this happens, you have to stop what you're doing, ask forgiveness from God and those in your care, make the necessary adjustments, and then get back on the right path. Remember, Courage must be rooted in truth and godly actions.

"In all your ways submit to him, and he will make your paths straight." (Proverbs 3:6)

7. Rally The Troops. When you're a leader, you have a team that will be looking for direction—especially when things aren't going well. In those moments you must be an encourager. In other words, give them the Courage to stand with you and to press forward.

"Therefore encourage one another and build each other up, just as in fact you are doing." (1 Thessalonians 5:11/NIV)

STUDY QUESTIONS

1. How do you define the word "Courage?"

2. Who are some people in your life or some people you have observed from afar that you would describe as Courageous? What makes those people Courageous?

3. What do you think is the connection between Confidence and Courage? Can you have one without the other? Explain.

4. Can you describe a situation where you felt like you lacked Courage? Why do you think that was the case?

5. When are some times when you have felt the most courageous? How were those times different from when you lacked Courage?

6. Looking back to the "Seven Keys To Courage," which ones have you struggled to enact as a leader?

7. What are some things you need to start doing today that will help you to become a more bold and Courageous leader?

FOLLOW THROUGH

• Write down your greatest fear, why it scares you, and your plan to overcome it.

• Read through and meditate on the scriptures found throughout this chapter. If you'd like to do some additional Bible study on Courage, here are some verses to get you started: Joshua 1:9, Proverbs 4:26-27, 1 Corinthians 16:13.

PRAYER

Lord, give me a strong, bold, and Courageous spirit. Continue to foster the Confidence within me that will allow me to follow Your lead, stay the course, and stand firm in what You have called me to do. I want to be a fearless leader for Your glory! Amen.

CHAPTER THREE: CHARACTER I
PREPARING ON THE INSIDE

"My old self has been crucified with Christ. It is no longer I who live, but Christ lives in me. So I live in this earthly body by trusting in the Son of God, who loved me and gave himself for me."
–Galatians 2:20 (NLT)

Character. It's a topic that is discussed daily in our schools, our churches, our businesses, our families, and our social media feeds. We talk about how to build Character, how to attain Character, how to have good Character, how to model Character, and so on.

But what does that really mean? Could it be possible that we've gotten this vitally important principle wrong? Is Character what we think it is, and do we really know where it comes from?

Over the next two chapters, we'll take a look at some of these questions from two perspectives: first from the internal side of the equation (the origins of Character) and then from the external side (how Character reveals itself).

Before we get started, however, let's define what Character means. In layman's terms, Character is simply who you are on the inside. It's what you do when no one is looking. It's a commitment to doing the right thing no matter the consequences. True lasting Character has one source, and it takes preparation for it to take root within the heart.

THE ONLY GOOD IN ME

In 1992, I was the head coach at George Washington University. That's when I first met an exceptional man named Jim Haney. He had just been hired as the executive director of the National Association of Basketball Coaches (NABC). I thought I knew what the word "Character" meant and how one attains character, but that all changed when I met Jim. Through his servant leadership and discipleship, I learned the truth about Character.

And it wasn't what I once thought.

Jim's dad was a preacher. He was raised on some basic Bible principles. When he was eight years old, his dad told him not to cheat, steal, or lie, and to try to adhere to the Ten Commandments. In Jim's mind, that's what it meant to have Character.

Jim never aspired to become a minister like his father, but he was eventually ordained while working in sports administration. As Jim committed himself to studying God's Word, he started to learn some counter cultural truths about the subject.

"In our world, there's all kinds of how to books on how important it is to have Character and the elements of having good Character," Jim once told me. "You don't earn Character. You don't grow character. Character is acquired through death to self, and Christ living in you. All other efforts to reflect character or be a good person or be a person of integrity are just a façade without dying to self and having Christ living in you. It's His Character."

Jim then quoted a Bible verse that often gets overlooked when we talk about Character. It's an incredible statement that Jesus made while answering a question from a man commonly referred to as the rich, young ruler. When wanting to know the requirements for getting into Heaven, he addressed Jesus as "Good Teacher."

"Why do you call me good?" Jesus answered. "No one is good—except God alone." (Luke 18:19/NIV)

With that scripture in mind, Jim made another profound statement: "The only good in me is God."

Now, to be honest, that didn't sound right to me at first. Most of the time, like so many of us, I believed that Character was something you earned, attained, or developed. Yes, there is preparation involved, and we'll discuss what that looks like later in this chapter, but true godly Character really has nothing to do with us at all. Instead, as Jim so eloquently explained, true godly Character comes from God through a relationship with His Son, Jesus.

That was something else Jim helped me better understand when he talked about the fallen nature of man that we are born with because of Adam and Eve's original sin in the Garden of Eden (Genesis 3). Because of that, God sent Jesus to earth as a man, where He lived a sinless life, showed us how to live godly lives, died on the cross for our sins, and defeated death when He was resurrected from the grave.

Jesus sacrificed everything so we could first and foremost have a relationship with God the Father. But He also did those things so we could live like He lived.

"To manifest the likeness of Christ and the Character of God, it's the Holy Spirit dwelling, and living, and abiding in us," Jim said. "True Character—Character that God defines—can only come through spending time with Him. It's spending time in the Word, spending time in prayer, and spending time in your thought life. It doesn't happen without absolute surrender."

Jim doesn't like talking about himself—especially when it comes to the topic of character. As much as I look up to him as a man of godly Character, he is always quick to point out that he's only human and makes mistakes every day. That might be true, but I'm certainly thankful that there are men like him that I can look up to as an example of what true character looks like from the inside out.

PREPARATION IN THE PALACE

I hope you have someone in your life like Jim who is a living, breathing example of true, godly Character. If you don't, that's okay, because the Bible has some wonderful examples from which we can learn. Chief among them is a man named Daniel. There's an entire Old Testament book that bears his name, and it gives us insight into the source of internal Character and how it reveals itself externally.

Daniel was one of the best and brightest young noblemen from the nation of Judah. When the Babylonians conquered Jerusalem, he and several others were taken from their homeland to serve King Nebuchadnezzar. Even before his arrival, Daniel had been prepared for the many tests that he was about to face.

First of all, he loved God and had a heart for doing what was right. Secondly, he was trained in the ways of the Lord and followed Jewish law. Thirdly, Daniel had learned to pray daily—even in his youth. All of these things created a foundation of godly principles upon which he could draw from at any given moment. Daniel knew God's voice and when He was present. Character meant something to him, and it was something worth protecting.

It wasn't long before Daniel and his three closest friends (Shadrach, Meshack, and Abednego) faced their first big test. The Hebrews were to partake of the king's table each day while being trained to enter his service, but this would mean defiling themselves with royal food and wine. Daniel boldly asked the chief official if he and his three friends could instead eat vegetables and drink water. Although the official was afraid he would anger the king, he accepted

Daniel's ten day challenge to compare their appearance to the appearance of the other young men.

At the end of the ten days, Daniel and the others looked healthier, and God blessed them with "knowledge, aptitude for learning, and wisdom. Daniel also could understand all kinds of visions and dreams." (Daniel 1:17/ISV)

Even though many others decided to go along with the king's orders, Daniel stood out because of his Character and his ability to stand by his convictions, which brings us back to the first two C's we discussed: Confidence and Courage. He had <u>Confidence</u> because A) he knew he belonged to God and B) he knew he had a purpose for being in the palace. Then, because of that Confidence, he had the <u>Courage</u> to make a decision that kept his <u>Character</u> intact. It's amazing how each of those principles worked in concert together to produce incredible and inspirational results. The same is true today in our lives.

FROM THE TEMPLE TO THE WILDERNESS

Earlier in this chapter, we talked about a meeting between Jesus and a rich, young ruler. It must have been strange to hear Jesus say that no one but God is truly good. The wealthy man along with countless others had witnessed Jesus teaching and performing miracles. Surely Jesus was good.

It's even stranger for us to read those words from Jesus, because we know something about Him that the rich, young ruler didn't fully understand. Jesus was in fact the Son of God. He would prove that to be true with His death and resurrection.

So how do we reconcile Jesus' words in Luke 18:19? We can do that when we realize that Jesus was fully man and fully God at the same time. In that moment, Jesus was speaking as a man. Yes, He was perfect and sinless, but here's what He was acknowledging: the only reason He was good was because God was in Him, and that's the point.

Even when we accept Christ as our Savior and make Him Lord of our life, we still have to deal with our human nature, and that's where God living inside of us comes into play. That's why the Holy Spirit must be actively involved in our lives if we're going to be a leader with true Character.

That's not all we learn about the subject from Jesus. In fact, you can see how He set an example for us as far back as His childhood. In Luke 2, we read that Jesus was "filled with wisdom" (v. 40), which indicates that just like all Hebrew boys, He was studying the scriptures. Then, on a trip to Jerusalem for the Feast of the Passover, something remarkable happened. Jesus was twelve years old at the time when His parents unknowingly left Him behind.

"Thinking he was in their company, they traveled on for a day. Then they began looking for him among their relative and friends. When they did not find him, they went back to Jerusalem to look for him. After three days they found him in the temple courts, sitting among the teachers, listening to them and asking them questions. Everyone who heard him was amazed at his understanding and his answers. When his parents saw him, they were astonished. His mother said to him, 'Son, why have you treated us like this? Your father and I have been anxiously searching for you.' 'Why were you searching for me?' he asked. 'Didn't you know I had to be in my Father's house?'" (Luke 2:44-50/NIV)

Mary and Joseph didn't understand what Jesus was saying. I'm sure much later on they did. For us reading the story today, we have the advantage of knowing how it ends and how this was just a foreshadowing of what Jesus would be doing throughout His ministry.

But even as He prepared to launch His ministry about twenty years later, there was still some preparation that needed to take place. It was in the wilderness just outside of Jerusalem where Jesus spent forty days and forty nights fasting and praying. Jesus knew that His Character would be tested and the only way He could be completely ready was to spend time communicating with God.

In His weakest state, the Devil took his best shot at taking down Jesus' ministry before it had even begun. The Devil presented three temptations that you can read about in Matthew 4:1-11, but on all three occasions, Jesus had the internal Character that allowed Him to resist.

Jesus' example didn't stop there. Throughout the four gospels, there are many times when we read about how He took time to study and pray (Mark 1:35, Luke 5:16, etc.). Even though Jesus wanted to reach the masses, He even had to get away from the crowds so He could be alone with God.

At the end of the day, however, it was all about surrender. Jesus gave Himself over to God's will and allowed the Father's Character to manifest in His heart. If you want to have Character, that's where it has to start.

SEVEN KEYS TO INTERNAL CHARACTER (OR PREPARING IT ON THE INSIDE)

Internal Character only happens when there is an absolute and total dependence on God. As He reveals Himself to us, that true, godly Character will become a part of who we are. Here are seven keys that are necessary as you go through this process:

1. Study The Word. Immerse yourself in the truth. You can't have true Character until you change your thoughts, and your thoughts have to be based upon God's Word.

"I have hidden your word in my heart that I might not sin against you." (Psalm 119:11/NIV)

2. Spend Time In Prayer. Ask God for help, and listen for His answers. Your goal should be uninterrupted spiritual intimacy with God. You may not always feel as close as you'd like, but make the effort, and He will bless you for it.

"The LORD is near to all who call on him, to all who call on him in truth; he hears their cry and saves them." (Psalm 145:18-19/NIV)

3. Get Dressed Up. You have some powerful weapons and protections at your disposal that will help strengthen the godly Character that is developing inside of you. Put them on and use them every day.

"Finally, be strong in the Lord and in his mighty power. Put on the full armor of God, so that you can take your stand against the devil's schemes. For our struggle is not against flesh and blood, but against the rulers, against the authorities, against the powers of this dark world and against the spiritual forces of evil in the heavenly realms. Therefore put on the full armor of God, so that when the day of evil comes, you may be able to stand your ground, and after you have

done everything, to stand. Stand firm then, with <u>the belt of truth</u> buckled around your waist, with <u>the breastplate of righteousness</u> in place, and with your feet fitted with the readiness that comes <u>from the gospel of peace</u>. In addition to all this, take up <u>the shield of faith</u>, with which you can extinguish all the flaming arrows of the evil one. Take <u>the helmet of salvation</u> and the sword of the Spirit, which is <u>the word of God</u>. And pray in the Spirit on all occasions with all kinds of prayers and requests. With this in mind, be alert and always keep on praying for all the Lord's people." (Ephesians 6:10-18/NIV)

4. Make Honest Self-Evaluations. Know your strengths, and more importantly, know your weaknesses. Being honest with yourself is a very important step in the process that will allow you to navigate the difficult choices in life that you will face. If you have any blind spots and aren't sure of your weaknesses, ask the Holy Spirit to reveal them to you.

"Search me, O God, and know my heart; test me and know my anxious thoughts. Point out anything in me that offends you, and lead me along the path of everlasting life." (Psalm 139:23-24/NLT)

5. Don't Get Amnesia. Don't forget where you came from and where your strength of Character comes from. This is much easier to do when you've bathed yourself in God's Word and when you've been consistent in your prayer life.

"For it is by grace you have been saved, through faith—and this is not from yourselves, it is the gift of God—not by works, so that no one can boast. For we are God's handiwork, created in Christ Jesus to do good works, which God prepared in advance for us to do." (Ephesians 2:8-10/NIV)

6. Make Calculated Choices. This means surrounding yourself with people that have good Character (as we saw in Daniel's story) and making sure that you aren't allowing ungodly ideas and thoughts to interfere with what the Holy Spirit is trying to accomplish in your heart. It's also important to get rid of the negativity around you and separate yourself from the people that are pulling you down.

"Do not be misled: Bad company corrupts good character." (1 Corinthians 15:33/NIV)

7. Submit To The Spirit. Speaking of the Holy Spirit, becoming a leader with godly Character ultimately comes down to listening to that still, small voice as it leads you down a path of righteousness and away from those things that can bring you down.

"If you love me, obey my commandments. And I will ask the Father, and he will give you another Advocate, who will never leave you. He is the Holy Spirit, who leads into all truth. The world cannot receive him, because it isn't looking for him and doesn't recognize him. But you know him, because he lives with you now and later will be in you. (John 14:15-17/NLT)

STUDY QUESTIONS

1. How do you define Character? How is your definition similar or different from how today's culture generally defines Character?

2. Who are some people in your life or some people you've observed that you would say have good Character? Explain.

3. Read Luke 18:19. What is your initial reaction to reading Jesus' claim that there is no one good but God? Does that affirm or change your opinion of the kind of Character you have?

4. What part do you think preparation plays in the development of Character? Which of the areas discussed (prayer, Bible study, following the Spirit, etc.) do you find most helpful? Which of the areas discussed do you struggle to make an active part of your daily routine?

5. How often do you evaluate your strengths and weaknesses? How do you think knowing those things about yourself could be valuable in developing Character?

6. What are some calculated choices that you have made that might help or hinder your ability to have good Character?

7. Of the seven keys listed, which ones do you need to do a better job of intentionally implementing in your life? How do you think doing so would strengthen your internal Character?

FOLLOW THROUGH

• Write down the name of a historical figure or someone you personally know that displays exceptional Character and some of the ways they demonstrated it.

• Commit to reading the Bible fifteen minutes daily so you can get to know the source of your Character (who and whose you are). If you do this, you will be able to read the entire Bible in 365 days!

• Read through and meditate on the scriptures found throughout this chapter. If you'd like to do some additional Bible study on building internal Character, here are some verses to get you started: Psalm 119:11, Psalm 139:23-24, Galatians 2:20.

PRAYER

Lord, I want to be filled with Your Character. Stir my heart every day to study Your word, spend time in prayer, and put on the full armor of God. Surround me with believers who will help me make choices, and most importantly, let Your Holy Spirit guide me every step of the way. It's all for Your glory. Amen.

CHAPTER FOUR: CHARACTER II
REVEALING IT ON THE OUTSIDE

"Whoever walks in integrity walks securely, but whoever takes crooked paths will be found out."
–Proverbs 10:9 (NIV)

As we talked about in chapter three, Character comes through a relationship with Christ and is fostered through daily preparation (Bible study and prayer) and submission to God's will. There comes a time, however, when Character will be put to the test.

Sometimes character is tested on the small stage. There might be a decision you have to make that seems insignificant at the time but has a big impact later on. And then there are those huge decisions that have an immediate impact on you and everyone around you.

In both cases, the people you lead are watching you. Why? Because leaders with high Character can be trusted and are easier to follow. That's why Character is such an important trait. You can't achieve long-term success if Character is not naturally flowing out of your thoughts, your words, and your actions.

FROM THE SHADOW OF THE VALLEY

In 1985, Jim Haney was the commissioner of the Missouri Valley Conference. One night he had an unusual dream. While standing on the top of a hill, he was suddenly whisked down into the valley below where he saw a rock garden with trees. There was one huge tree in particular that stood out because basketballs were growing on the branches. He woke up from the vivid dream, not fully understanding what it meant, but he knew there was something significant that God was trying to tell him.

When Jim left the MVC in 1992 to become the executive director of the NABC, his dream started to make sense. As he walked into the lobby of the hotel at his first Final Four, he clearly remembered seeing the place littered with empty beer cases. That's when the Holy Spirit spoke to him and convinced him that things needed to change. He now understood that God was calling him to use his influence and leadership to make a spiritual impact on the NCAA basketball coaching community.

Back then the Final Four consisted of three games to determine the NCAA basketball champion, business meetings, coaching clinics, and a lot of social events. It was a great way for coaches and their wives to unwind after a long season, renew old acquaintances, network, and have a great time.

But there was something missing, so Jim and his staff began scheduling ministry events with cooperation from organizations like Fellowship of Christian Athletes (FCA), Athletes in Action (AIA), American Family Coaches, the National Center For Fathering, and others. The Final Four became a family destination that included a Sunday non-denominational service that truly fed the body, mind, and soul of the attendees.

Jim also planted the seeds for Nation of Coaches and the Character Coach program, which ministers to coaches and players throughout the basketball season. He also organized a ministry board to oversee these operations and entrusted others to administrate his vision. He was never afraid to delegate because of the trust and faith that he had in people and the mighty God he served.

That's not the only thing Jim wasn't afraid to do. On many occasions, he would stand up at an event or a meeting and open with prayer. He knew everyone wasn't happy about the fact that he was praying, but his Christ-centered Character wouldn't allow him to stray from his convictions.

"I don't see that as me doing that," Jim told me. "I see that it's the Holy Spirit. My flesh wants to be politically correct. My flesh says, 'Just sit down and don't say anything about God.' So whose Character is it? It's not mine because I'm at war with the Holy Spirit. I have to let the Holy Spirit have His way."

Jim's Character has also manifested in the way he conducts NABC business. Not long after he became Executive Director, there was a potential boycott from the Black Coaches Association (BCA) that included some very influential head coaches such as John Thompson at Georgetown, George Raveling at USC, John Cheney at Temple, Nolan Richardson at Arkansas, and yours truly. We were upset about the NCAA's introduction of Prop 48, which raised entrance standards for college athletes based on SAT scores that were culturally and socio-economically biased.

I was so impressed at how Jim handled himself throughout that difficult circumstance. He never tried to manipulate the situation in his favor, and he always listened to what everyone had to say. I always appreciated how he was willing to go against the grain if necessary and never fell victim to political correctness. At the end of the day, Jim's calm and steady leadership style helped to diffuse the situation and avoid a boycott.

"My desire is to do the will of God, but I don't necessarily dwell upon what others might think about me," Jim added. "I'm a conduit of God to reveal Himself to bring direction. It doesn't have to be my voice. My only responsibility is to stand and say 'His will be done.'"

There's something profoundly rich about that statement. It's pretty challenging too. Exercising true, godly Character is ultimately about putting aside what you want and recognizing what God wants. The results may not always make everyone happy. In fact, there will rarely be a time when everyone will be completely satisfied with your leadership. But it won't matter in the end if your decisions are in line with God's will.

FROM THE PALACE TO THE PIT

When Daniel and his three Hebrew friends first arrived in Babylon, their Character was immediately tested when the king insisted that they partake of his royal food and wine. Although the other young men from Jerusalem caved to the pressure, Daniel, Shadrach, Meshach, and Abednego resisted the temptation to go against their beliefs. In turn, God blessed them with wisdom, strength, favor, and influence.

But the happy ending didn't last for long.

In Daniel 3, we read about one of the first big challenges to their Character. In that story, the three Hebrew children (as they are commonly called) found themselves front and center when King Nebuchadnezzar built an enormous, gold statue and commanded everyone in the land to worship it during a special dedication. If anyone refused to bow down and worship the statue, they would be thrown into a fiery furnace.

When the king's musicians began to play, everyone obeyed his orders and bowed down—everyone except for Shadrach, Meshach, and Abednego. Needless to say, Nebuchadnezzar was angry. He gave them one more chance to comply, but they stood firm in their convictions and refused to worship anyone but God. With that final refusal, the king ordered his guards to turn up the furnace seven times hotter. It was so hot that the guards were consumed as the Hebrews fell into the flames.

Miraculously, the young men survived, and the king spotted a fourth man in the furnace with them—a man that Nebuchadnezzar said appeared to look like the Son of God. After calling Shadrach, Meshach, and Abednego out of the fire, the king decreed that the people follow and acknowledge the one true God and then promoted them to higher levels of authority.

The Bible doesn't tell us where Daniel was during this time, but it's clear that his influence was evident in the way they handled the intense situation. In a moment of severe pressure, they took up the mantle and showed the king that their Character was real. Even more importantly, God was glorified, and the nation was turned because of their faithful leadership.

Daniel would face his own set of problems soon enough. A few years later, Darius the Mede, the King of Persia, took control of Babylon. By then, Daniel was one of the nation's most powerful men, but the other administrators were jealous and tried to dig up some dirt on him and have him removed. There was only one problem with that plan. Daniel had impeccable Character.

"They could find no corruption in him, because he was trustworthy and neither corrupt nor negligent." (Daniel 6:4b/NIV)

So they decided to set a trap. They knew the only way they could get him to break the law of the land was to create conflict with God's law. The administrators approached King Darius and convinced him to issue a law that would prohibit anyone from praying to anyone other than him. Anyone who disobeyed the law would be thrown into the lions' den.

In a moment of prideful excess, King Darius sent out the decree, and it was made known throughout the land. You might think that Daniel would simply wait it out. After all, it was just thirty days. Surely he could pray in private, or under his breath, or not at all. Why blow a good thing? He was a child of God, leading and influencing in a foreign land! There was only one problem with that notion. Daniel had impeccable Character.

"Now when Daniel learned that decree had been published, he went home to his upstairs room where the windows opened toward

Jerusalem. Three times a day he got down on his knees and prayed, giving thanks to his God, just as he done before." (Daniel 6/10/NIV)

Needless to say, Daniel's enemies were watching and waiting. They quickly reported the news to Darius who was immediately heartbroken. Daniel was his beloved advisor, but there was no way around it. Daniel was thrown into the lions' den. If you've attended Sunday School at any point in your childhood, you already know how this story ends. God sent an angel to shut the lions' mouths, and Daniel's life was spared.

Daniel was committed to righteousness. He was unwavering in his beliefs and confident that God was going to protect him. But even if the lions had devoured him in that pit, Daniel's Character would have remained unblemished. Nothing was going to stop Daniel from obeying God and fulfilling His purpose.

In both situations, internal Character was revealed when the fire was turned up and the lions were set to attack. Because of these young men's faithfulness, the Babylonian kings and the people turned to God. Daniel and the three Hebrews also became more influential. That's what happens when Character is tested and proven to be true, godly Character.

CHARACTER ASSASSINATION

When Jesus emerged from the wilderness after forty days and forty nights of fasting and praying, His Character remained intact, but it wasn't the last time it would be tested. Not much time passed during His ministry before a group of religious leaders called Pharisees took notice.

In the wilderness, the Devil was trying to ruin God's plan to redeem mankind before it could go into action. The Pharisees and the Sadducees, on the other hand, failed to recognize that Jesus was the Son of God. These elite groups that made up two of the three major Jewish sects were too busy trying to protect their traditions and their status as religious leaders, while defending their varying interpretations of the scriptures. Jesus and His message of love, grace, and hope along with His example of servant leadership was clearly a threat to their way of life.

To remove that threat, both groups engaged in one of the first century's most notable Character assassination attempts. They tried to trip up Jesus with trick questions. They hoped to catch Him making a contradictory statement or teaching something that didn't line up with Jewish law. And if they couldn't disqualify Him as a trusted leader, they would then create a false narrative that might cause the Roman authorities to view Him as a dangerous revolutionary figure.

Ultimately, they couldn't cause Jesus to stumble or compromise His Character despite the fact that He was "tempted in every way...yet he did not sin." (Hebrews 4:15/NIV)

In doing so, not only did He become the perfect sacrifice for *our* sins, He also showed us what it looks like to live with true, godly Character. We'll never be perfect like Jesus was, but we can certainly strive for perfection as we follow His example.

SEVEN KEYS TO EXTERNAL CHARACTER (OR REVEALING IT ON THE OUTSIDE)

As a leader, you will inevitably face opposition. Not everyone will agree with your decisions and some may even seek to take you out of your leadership position. Character is one of the biggest aspects of your life that will come under attack. That's why it's so important to make living with integrity a priority.

It's also important to remember what we discussed in chapter three—true, godly Character begins when you enter into a surrendered relationship with God through His Son, Jesus. From there, it's about staying in God's Word and communicating with him in prayer, and then committing to follow the Holy Spirit in every decision you make.

There are, however, steps you can take to allow that Character to manifest itself on a daily basis. With that in mind, here are seven keys to helping you maintain your integrity and become a principled leader:

1. Die To Self. This is simply a continuation of the submission that takes place when we ask Jesus to be the Lord of our lives. To do that, we have to daily decide to put Him first and ourselves last when making leadership decisions.

"Set your minds on things above, not on earthly things. ³For you died, and your life is now hidden with Christ in God." (Colossians 3:2-3/NIV)

2. Guard Your Heart. Negative emotions (and sometimes the pursuit of positive emotions) often get the best of us. Anger, jealousy, fear, doubt, guilt, frustration, sadness, and disappointment are just a few emotions that can cause us to use poor judgment when left unchecked.

"Guard your heart above all else, for it determines the course of your life." (Psalm 4:23/NIV)

3. Filter Your Thoughts. So much of our battle against temptation and compromise starts in the mind. That's why it's so important to protect our thought life from anything that might take us off course and steer us away from the truth of God's Word.

"And now, dear brothers and sisters, one final thing. Fix your thoughts on what is true, and honorable, and right, and pure, and lovely, and admirable. Think about things that are excellent and worthy of praise." (Philippians 4:8/NLT)

4. Be Patient. Give situations time to unfold. Don't rush God. This is especially true when you are going through trials and temptations or even being persecuted for doing the right thing. God will use the bad around you to build up the good inside of you.

"We also have joy with our troubles, because we know that these troubles produce patience. And patience produces character, and character produces hope." (Romans 5:3-4/NCV)

5. Stay Focused. Don't let the world distract you from your mission. Don't let the world talk you out believing in truth. Singular focus is an important attribute that will help you make wise decisions and keep your character intact.

"Let your eyes look straight ahead; fix your gaze directly before you." (Proverbs 4:25/NIV)

6. Avoid The Traps. Don't put yourself in bad situations or put yourself in a position where you can easily pick up old, destructive habits. Be aware that the Devil is looking to take you out and will try to bring back your past mistakes to do just that.

"You were taught, with regard to your former way of life, to put off your old self, which is being corrupted by its deceitful desires; to be made new in the attitude of your minds; and to put on the new self, created to be like God in true righteousness and holiness." (Ephesians 4:22-24)

7. Call For Help. It's going to happen eventually. You're going to have those moments where you feel overwhelmed and it seems like everything or everyone is against you. Sometimes you just need to cry out to God for a rescue. That help might come in the form of inner peace, an escape from trouble, or some wise counsel from a trusted friend. Whatever you do, don't try to go it alone. No matter what your status in life might be, all leaders need to rely on God and His people for strength, comfort, and direction.

"The LORD is my rock, my fortress and my deliverer;
my God is my rock, in whom I take refuge,
my shield and the horn of my salvation, my stronghold.
I called to the LORD, who is worthy of praise,
and I have been saved from my enemies." (Psalm 18:2-3/NIV)

STUDY QUESTIONS

1. Can you describe a time when you felt like your Character has been significantly tested? Would you say you passed or failed that test? Explain.

2. Jim Haney talks about the importance of knowing God's will as it relates to Character. What do you think that means? Can you think of a time when knowing God's will for your life impacted your actions and revealed your Character?

3. How would you define "Character assassination?" What are some examples that you've seen in the public square or in your personal life? Why do you think Character assassination is such an effective way to negatively impact leadership?

4. What are some things that you personally do to protect your Character as a leader? What are some specific ways that those things have been helpful?

5. What are some key principles you can take away from reading about how Jesus dealt with people attacking His Character?

6. Of the seven keys to external Character, which ones do you feel like you've done a good job of implementing? Which ones have you struggled to apply to your life and why?

7. What are some things you need to start doing today that will help you better make decisions that reflect the true, godly Character that resides within your heart as a Christian leader?

FOLLOW THROUGH

• Think of a time when you exhibited good Character. Then, think of a time when you exhibited bad Character. Reflect on what you learned from both situations.

• Commit the following poem to memory:

> *Watch your thoughts—they become words.*
> *Watch your words—they become actions.*
> *Watch your actions—they become habits.*
> *Watch your habits—they become your character.*
> *Watch your character—it becomes your identity.*

• Per the action item in the previous chapter, continue to read the Bible fifteen minutes daily in the Word.

• Read through and meditate on the scriptures found throughout this chapter. If you'd like to do some additional Bible study on exhibiting external Character, here are some verses to get you started: Proverbs 10:9, Philippians 4:8, Colossians 3:2-3.

PRAYER

Lord, I surrender my heart to You. Help me to die daily to myself, and allow You to shape me in the image of Christ. Guard my heart from sinful thoughts and behaviors. Help me avoid the traps that the enemy has set for me. You are my rock and my fortress. I'm trusting in You and only You to keep my Character intact. Amen.

CHAPTER FIVE: COMMITMENT
GIVING YOUR ALL

"So let's not get tired of doing what is good. At just the right time we will reap a harvest of blessing if we don't give up."
–Galatians 6:9 (NLT)

Commitment. It's a word that is used often in our world but sadly abandoned or discarded when things get tough. Just like Courage is a by-product of Confidence, Commitment is a by-product of Character. When you are strong in Character, you can stay committed to the people in your life. You can stay committed to those whom you are leading. You can stay committed to the cause. You can stay committed to serving the purpose to which God has called you.

But without Character, Commitment becomes a fleeting thought that quickly evaporates at the first hint of adversity. That's why modern day leadership is suffering—because without true, godly Character, unshakeable Commitment will rarely last.

SACRIFICIAL LOVE

Throughout my life, Commitment has never been in short supply thanks to some special people like Stretch Headley, Ms. Key, Coach Dick Dukeshire, my brother Richard, my sister Trudy, and of course my mom, Dorothy. But no one has been more committed to me than my wife, Connie.

Her first recollection of me was when I was ten years old. That's when I used to terrorize the girls in the Central Square Theater on Saturday afternoons—or so she says. It took me a while longer to notice her, ninth grade to be exact. That's when we moved four blocks to 135 River Street. She lived right next door at 133 River Street.

Connie caught my eye immediately. She always carried herself in a very dignified manner. She had an air of Confidence and style. She also happened to be very attractive. The distance between our houses was less than twenty feet. My mom couldn't understand why we talked on the phone all the time.

"Why don't you just open your window?" she wondered out loud.

Those conversations turned into long walks, and those long walks turned into a dating relationship. We were together throughout high school, and she became a big part of my academic life at Northeastern. I've often said that she should have walked on the stage at The Boston Garden with me to get my diploma. She probably did more work than I did. Connie helped me organize and type my papers. She studied with me. She was completely committed to my personal and educational growth.

When we got married, we were both working. I was a teacher and she was a buyer for Filene's, a department store in Boston. Our plan was to save some money before starting a family. The Vietnam War changed everything. In 1968, a clerk from City Hall named Hellen Hollum advised us to speed up our plan in order to avoid being drafted. Connie was shocked to hear the news, but her Commitment to me and to our future paved the way for our first child, Michael Delaney Jarvis II.

Throughout my coaching career, Connie encouraged me and motivated me to do and be my best. She always made me feel like I was capable of doing special things. Then, when it came time to make sacrificial decisions—like starting a family years earlier than planned—Connie was always willing to do what needed to be done.

Another example was in 1990 when George Washington University asked me to be their head coach. At the time, Connie had gone back to school for her undergraduate degree at Emmanuel College. She was toward the top of the class and had been accepted into Boston University's prestigious counseling program. Instead, she gave up an incredible opportunity and stayed committed to her family. At GW, however, Connie earned a Master's degree in Education and Human Development.

No matter where I coached, Connie was an integral part of the team. She didn't love basketball, or any sports for that matter, but she tolerated them because she loved me and was totally committed to me and my chosen profession. Connie used her ability to read people and was the unofficial counselor and psychologist for the team. She also used her talents and skills as a cook to feed and nurture the players. Connie fulfilled all of those roles with excellence, because she believed that her number one role was to love and support her husband.

In 1998, I was named head coach at St. John's University in Queens, New York. When we first moved there, we lived in Manhattan while looking for a home closer to the school. Connie was intimidated by the city and rarely ventured out of the apartment. It was a wild and crazy place—a place we loved to visit but never aspired to live in. Connie eventually got over that fear. By the time we left New York, she drove her car like she was a taxi cab driver. Nothing could shake her.

Within that story, however, there was a very dark time. On the surface, everything seemed to be perfect. We had some incredible highs, like being three points away from the Final Four in 1999, winning the Big East Tournament in 2000, and capturing the 2003 National Invitational Tournament title. Connie was very active in the community and received several honors including the Big Apple Award from Mayor Michael Bloomberg.

Then, she lost her mother, her stepfather, and her sister. My brother, Richard, also passed during that time. To make matters worse, coaching in New York consumed my life. Almost all of my time was devoted to recruiting, designing offenses and defenses and, of course, winning games. I was also taking care of media responsibilities and living out my dream as a big name coach in the Big East. Because of the blinders I was wearing, I didn't see what was happening to my incredible wife. The pressure and crowd negativity were getting to her. She had a tough time sleeping at night, started losing weight, and even lost her appetite for shopping.

In December 2003, it all came crumbling down. Our team got off to a tough 2-4 start and the "Fire Jarvis" chants quickly followed. At the same time, my contract extension talks had grown contentious because of an adversarial relationship between my agent and the university's president.

Connie was struggling with it all. She was not only concerned about my future, but also about her son's future. Mike Jr. was on my staff, and his coaching career was in jeopardy along with mine. Connie was pressed to the point where she had a nervous breakdown. It's a sobering thought when I realize what could have happened if I had received a contract extension and not been fired. Connie probably wouldn't be alive today, and all the wins and all the money in the world could not have compensated for her loss.

In the spring of 2004, we left New York and moved to Boca Raton, Florida. I took a job with ESPN as an analyst, but Connie was more concerned about finding a church home. Through divine intervention, we ended up at Spanish River Community Church and met Pastor David Nicholas, the man who led me to Christ and changed my life forever.

Connie then encouraged me to get back into coaching, and I took a job at Florida Atlantic University. She was just as committed to the program during that six-year tenure as she had been everywhere else we had traveled. But this time, we both had renewed purpose. Thank God Connie put her emotional and physical health on the line during those darkest times in New York. Her Commitment to me literally saved my life.

SACRIFICIAL LEGACY

In the Old Testament, there's a different kind of love story that serves as another example of Commitment. It all started with a young, Jewish woman named Esther. The entire account can be found in the book that shares her name, but here's a paraphrased glimpse into how one person's Commitment saved an entire nation.

Esther lived in a time when the Jewish people had been driven out of their homeland and exiled to a land called Persia (or Babylon). King Xerxes ruled the nation alongside Queen Vashti. When Vashti refused to appear before Xerxes at a party, an advisor named Haman urged the king to her put to death.

Xerxes needed a new queen, so he decreed a search for the most beautiful woman who would become his bride. The King's men discovered Esther, and, after being chosen over several others, she was indeed married to Xerxes and declared Persia's queen. It was an incredible Commitment for this young lady to make. Esther had to leave her community and enter into a marital relationship with a stranger, but she had been prepared for the moment thanks to her uncle and mentor, a Jewish leader named Mordecai.

Eventually, tensions arose between Haman and Mordecai to the point that Haman hatched a plot to have the entire Jewish population killed. This put Esther in a very difficult place. She could remain silent and preserve her life, or she could risk it all in an effort to save her people. Ultimately, it was the words of her uncle that gave her the courage to stay committed to her people.

"Do not think that because you are in the king's house you alone of all the Jews will escape. For if you remain silent at this time,

relief and deliverance for the Jews will arise from another place, but you and your father's family will perish. And who knows but that you have come to your royal position for such a time as this?" (Esther 4:13-14/NIV)

Esther created her own plan to counter Haman's evil actions and showed strength and courageous Commitment in order to go through with it. She knew she might die trying but refused to take her eyes off the big picture. Because Esther had faith and trusted God for the outcome, a nation was saved.

SACRIFICIAL LIFE

There is no greater example of committed leadership than in the life of Christ. But what if I told you that His arrival doesn't happen without one young girl who was willing to take on a courageous Commitment of her own? Her name was Mary, and her story is an example of how Commitment can save the world.

Most historians believe that Mary was in her mid-teens when she was betrothed (or engaged) to a young man named Joseph. But something miraculous happened before her marriage ceremony was completed. The angel Gabriel appeared to her and told her that she would give birth to a child that she would name Jesus. At this point, Mary had a choice. She could reject her assignment, or she could make a life-altering Commitment that would take Courage and strength of Character.

Mary understood what this Commitment meant. She was risking her relationship with Joseph. She was risking rejection from her family. She was even risking punishment for what would have been perceived as a sinful act on her part. At the very least, she risked embarrassment and humiliation. None of that mattered, because she trusted God.

"I am the LORD's servant," Mary answered. "May your word to me be fulfilled." (Luke 1:38).

Even still, Mary had to deal with what a lot of people can't deal with—public opinion. People were going to think she was having a baby out of wedlock. There was a stigma that came with that, but her relationship with God far outweighed the fear and doubt she must have been facing.

Mary had the toughest decision to make, but she didn't have to do it alone. At first, Joseph was going to quietly end the engagement when he learned she was pregnant, but after an angel visited him, he too was convinced that God's hand was in it all. Mary also had the support of her cousin, Elizabeth, who took her in for three months and gave her encouragement and support. Mary's story shows us why it's so important to have a good team around us when making a significant commitment.

But it didn't end with the birth of Jesus in Bethlehem. No, it was just the beginning. Mary and Joseph protected Him when Herod sought to murder all of the male, Jewish infants. She worried about Him when He was separated from the family while spending time in the temple. Mary was there when Jesus worked His first miracle at a wedding where He turned water into wine, and she continued to follow Him throughout His ministry.

Sadly, as recorded in John 19, Mary was also there when Jesus, a sinless, perfect man, was brutally tortured and then crucified. She was one of three others—Mary of Clopas, Mary Magdalene, and John—who stood at the foot of the cross until Jesus took His last breath. It's hard to imagine how Mary must have felt as her son's limp, bloodied body was taken down and wrapped for burial. Perhaps she questioned the Commitment she had made as a teenage girl. Perhaps she questioned how something so awful could be part of God's plan. Or perhaps she was simply filled with grief as her child of promise was placed inside a tomb and sealed with a heavy stone.

Thankfully, that grief didn't last for long. As the Bible records in Luke 24, Jesus was raised from the dead three days later and appeared to His disciples and several other followers including His mother, Mary. Then, after Jesus ascended back to Heaven, Mary was the only one, other than the eleven apostles, mentioned in Acts 1 when the Holy Spirit visited them in the upper room.

Mary was there at every stage of God's plan. She brought Jesus into the world through a miraculous, virgin birth. She watched Him grow into a man whose ministry impact continues to be felt today. She watched Him suffer and die, and then resurrected from the dead. And finally, she was there when God sent His Holy Spirit to serve as the catalyst for the birth of His Church.

Just like Mary, when we are Committed to the cause to which God has called us, we will experience joy, pain, and everything in between. But as long as we understand the big picture, we will ultimately receive incredible blessings for staying true to His greater purpose. That's what a sacrificial legacy looks like.

SEVEN KEYS TO COMMITMENT (OR GIVING YOUR ALL)

All three of these stories show what happens when a person exercises committed leadership. Connie's Commitment to me eventually led me to Christ. Esther's Commitment to her people saved the Jewish population from extinction. Mary's Commitment to God's plan ushered Jesus and His history-changing message into the world. Great victories happen when we stay committed to the plan.

Here are seven biblical keys to becoming a more committed leader:

1. Recognize The Need. Someone in your life needs your Commitment, and that someone might be you. Commit yourself to spiritual and personal growth first. From there, look around and see who needs you most, whether it's your immediate family, your extended family, your friends, your neighbors, your church, or your community.

"Bear one another's burdens, and so fulfill the law of Christ." (Galatians 6:2/ESV)

2. Check Your Heart. Make sure you have pure motives. Committing to someone or something must first be based on what God has called you to do. Equally important is walking out that Commitment, not for the blessings you will receive, but out of obedience to God and as a pure act of service to others.

"For the LORD searches every heart and understands every desire and every thought. If you seek him, he will be found by you; but if you forsake him, he will reject you forever." (2 Chronicles 28:9b/NIV)

3. Step Up To The Plate. It's one thing to recognize the need and to have a pure heart, but those things don't matter unless you turn it into action. Don't sit back and wait for the perfect time to commit to someone else.

"Do not withhold from those to whom it is due, when it is in your power to act." (Proverbs 3:27/NIV)

4. Go All In. When you Commit yourself to someone or something, do it wholeheartedly and with everything you have. Be consistent and give your best effort.

"Whatever you do, work at it with all your heart, as working for the Lord, not for human masters, since you know that you will receive an inheritance from the Lord as a reward. It is the Lord Christ you are serving." (Colossians 3:23-24/NIV)

5. Set Boundaries. People who are Committed can often become magnets for needy people. But remember, you can only do so much. Therefore, sometimes you have to say no. Even Jesus took time to get away from the people who needed Him.

"Yet the news about him spread all the more, so that crowds of people came to hear him and to be healed of their sicknesses. But Jesus often withdrew to lonely places and prayed." (Luke 5:15-16/NIV)

6. Don't Over Commit. Know your limits. Don't take on too much at once. The more you try to do, the less effective you will become. If you're not sure whether or not you should Commit to something, God's Word gives us some good advice on how to proceed:

"It is better to say nothing than to make a promise and not keep it." (Ecclesiastes 5:5/NLT)

7. Don't Waver. Commitment isn't easy. There will be adversity. Sometimes those you're trying to help will push you away. Sometimes you'll make mistakes in the middle of acting on that Commitment. But don't give up. You may not see the results right away, but God will bless you for your faithfulness.

"So let's not get tired of doing what is good. At just the right time we will reap a harvest of blessing if we don't give up." (Galatians 6:9/NLT)

STUDY QUESTIONS

1. What does the word "Commitment" mean to you?

2. Who are some people that have been Committed to you? How do you think your life would be different if they hadn't been fully Committed?

3. What are some common hindrances to Commitment? Which of those hindrances have kept you from being more consistent in your Commitments?

4. Are you able to personally relate to any aspects of the three stories discussed in this chapter? Explain.

5. In each of these stories, the main characters were required to sacrifice something in order to fulfill their Commitment. What is the most difficult aspect of sacrifice for you personally?

6. Of the seven keys to Commitment, which would you say have helped you be a more Committed leader? Which ones have you struggled to live out?

7. What are some things you need to sacrifice that will help you become a more Committed leader (in your family, at your school, at your job, at your church, etc.)?

FOLLOW THROUGH

• Make a twenty-one day Commitment to give up something—a bad habit such as fast food, alcohol, smoking, negative online activity, foul language, gossip, etc., and replace it with something positive or life affirming.

• Write a letter to, visit, or call someone who's Commitment has been important to you (i.e. spouse, parent, grandparent, sibling, friend, coach, teacher, co-worker, etc.).

• Read through and meditate on the scriptures found throughout this chapter. If you'd like to do some additional Bible study on Commitment, here are some verses to get you started: Proverbs 3:27, Galatians 6:2, Galatians 6:9.

PRAYER

Lord, allow me to see the world around me with Your eyes. I want to help fulfill the needs of those closest to me, those in my community, and those that I cannot see. Purify my motives, and give me the strength to be committed to whatever causes You call me to pursue. Let those that I help see Jesus in me. Amen.

CHAPTER SIX: COMMUNICATION I
SPEAKING TO YOUR TEAM

"The tongue can bring death or life; those who love to talk will reap the consequences."
–Proverbs 18:21 (NLT)

In the first five chapters, we've talked about four foundational elements that all leaders must have: Confidence (chapter one), Courage (chapter two), Character (chapters three and four), and Commitment (chapter five). For the next six chapters, we're going to pivot toward some tools that can fine-tune your leadership efforts. Let's start with the vitally important concept of Communication.

Communication is something we do every day, but how often do we think about the messages we are sending with our words and our actions? It doesn't matter if you are in charge of leading one person or a thousand people, Communication is one of the most important skills that one needs in order to be an effective leader.

In chapter seven, we'll talk about how to communicate a message to an external audience, but first we need to address the importance of internal (or interpersonal) Communication. In other words, how can you motivate your team, get them on the same page, and prepare them to take that message outside of your organization's four walls?

WISE WORDS FROM A LEGEND

My first year as head coach at Cambridge Rindge and Latin High School was one of the toughest seasons in my entire forty-six-year career. Anything less than a state championship was going to be considered a failure.

We finished the regular season undefeated, and expectations for a championship were off the charts. As far as the community was concerned, there was no way we could lose. Patrick Ewing was only a sophomore, but he was already dominating in the paint and anchoring one of the top ten teams in the country.

In the semifinal game against Boston Latin and its all-American candidate, Paul Little, however, things weren't going as planned. We were heavily favored to win, but we weren't playing up to our usual standards. I could see the whole season and my coaching career disappearing before my very eyes.

At halftime, I looked up at the scoreboard and couldn't believe what I was seeing. The Mighty Warriors of CRLS were trailing by twelve points and the sellout crowd of 13,909 fans that filled The Boston Garden were just as shocked as I was. To make matters worse, my coaching hero Red Auerbach of the Boston Celtics was sitting in the stands with one of his former players, John Thompson, who was now the head coach at Georgetown University.

My anger grew with every step as I walked toward the locker room. Those poor kids were going to get it. I was going to rip into them and motivate them to play the way I knew they could play.

However, just before I could open the locker room door, an old friend came out of nowhere and gently grabbed my arm. It was Rindge Jefferson, my first basketball coach and one of my trusted mentors. He ran the Cambridge Community Center, which was on Howard Street where I lived. Rindge was an incredible teacher and one of the neighborhood's true leaders. He gave me a chance to play when I was the little, chubby kid they called "Crisco." He mentored me and disciplined me when I couldn't control my mouth. I had nothing but love for Rindge and everything he had done for me.

Naturally, I stopped and listened to what he had to say, and it took me by surprise.

"Oh Mike!" He smiled as he wrapped his arm around my shoulders. "I'm so proud of you! You're doing such an incredible job with the kids."

Rindge's words took me back to the Community Center when he was teaching, coaching, and loving me and my buddies.

"Listen, I know you're not happy with the kids and the way they're playing. They might be playing *too* hard. I think they want to win more for you than anything. These kids love you, and they probably think they need to win in order for you to keep your job. Be positive, be gentle, and everything will work out. Keep that in mind before you walk through that door."

I didn't see what Rindge saw. All I saw was their mistakes and the score. It hadn't crossed my mind that they were overplaying and maybe feeling the weight of the community's expectations. My love and respect for Rindge, and what he said, changed my perspective and helped me change my approach and the words I would use during my halftime talk.

Instead of ranting and raving, I calmly took off my suit jacket, loosened my tie, and put on the biggest smile I could find. I then told the guys that I believed in them and their ability. I told them to refocus and relax, and to continue trusting one another, and how much fun they were going to have cutting down the nets in The Boston Garden.

I would have done things a lot differently if I hadn't listened to Rindge. If I had gone in there and said what I was going to say, I don't think we would have won that game. Instead, a change of heart and a change of message relieved the intense pressure those kids were feeling and gave them the freedom to play basketball and have fun doing it.

We came from behind to win the game and went on to win the first of three consecutive state titles while compiling an almost perfect record of 77-1. The lessons I learned that day, however, were much more valuable.

THE NIGHT THEY TURNED OUT THE LIGHTS

After seven years at Cambridge, I made the leap to the college ranks at Boston University where I spent five seasons. From there, I went to George Washington University and experienced the highly competitive Atlantic 10 Conference, which at the time, featured great coaches such as John Calipari (the University of Massachusetts) and John Cheney (Temple University).

As I got deeper into my career, Rindge Jefferson's words slowly faded from my memory. With each step, I became more consumed with winning. The competitive mindset sometimes had a negative impact on the way I communicated to my team.

During the 1993 conference season, we had a game at St. Joseph's University in Philadelphia where they played in a bandbox of a gym called Hagan Arena. I felt confident heading into the matchup. We had won eight of our last nine games and we were well prepared. The team played great, but we lost, 74-73, on a heartbreaking buzzer beater.

I should have been proud of the fact that we were that close, but instead, I was very disappointed, because I knew we could have won. There were two players in particular that didn't perform to their capabilities at some key moments in the contest. So I gave them riot act one, two, and three. I must have broken down every possession and analyzed every player. I was very angry. I had made it all about me. I wanted the victory more for myself than I wanted it for the team. I went on and on and on. I asked my assistants for their opinions, and they went on and on and on. The poor players just took it.

Two hours later, it was midnight, and we were still sitting there in that locker room. We also had to get on the bus and take a two hour drive back to Washington D.C. I probably would have kept going if the custodian hadn't shut the lights out. I'm sure the players were thankful that he did. On the way home, we didn't make our customary stop for a late night snack. Instead, we all sat in complete silence.

I never had another postgame talk that went that long, but I had many that went longer than necessary. Even toward the end of my coaching career, I'm sure that many of my halftime and postgame remarks felt more like a wake. If only I had remembered the lessons Rindge Jefferson taught me about how much effect our words can have on the final outcome.

THE GREAT COMMUNICATOR

When Jesus came to our world, he did so as the Son of God in human form. His primary objective was to reconcile man back to God through His death and resurrection. He also had the mission of delivering God's message to Earth. But before He could embark on that mission, He needed to build a team of willing disciples who would follow Him and learn from Him.

Jesus had to get this right. The future of mankind depended on it. And even though His disciples didn't quite understand what was happening in the moment, those twelve men (minus Judas, who later betrayed Jesus) would eventually take the gospel of faith, hope, and love to every corner of civilization. To that end, over a period of three and a half years, the greatest communicator of all time diligently taught them how to communicate that message to the masses.

So how did Jesus do it? His formula was quite simple. He asked questions. He listened to their answers. He broke things down (in their language). And He repeated Himself until it finally clicked.

Asking questions was one of Jesus' most effective ways to communicate biblical truths to the disciples. In fact, between the four Gospels—Matthew, Mark, Luke, and John—He asked over one hundred questions, and many of them were directed at His disciples. That might seem strange coming from the Son of God. After all, He already knew the answers. But the purpose behind those questions was to get their responses so He could, in turn, teach them memorable lessons about His message.

Sometimes their answers were contrived and based on a lack of understanding—like the time Jesus asked Peter three times if he loved Him. Peter, of course, said yes all three times to which Jesus responded, "Feed my lambs," "Take care of my sheep," and "Feed my sheep." Peter was bothered that Jesus didn't seem to believe him, but Jesus was trying to make a bigger point that true love was more than words and only proven through actions.

Other times their answers opened the door for an "aha" moment—like the time Jesus asked the disciples a two-part question:

"Who do people say the Son of man is?"

They replied, "Some say John the Baptist; others say Elijah; and still others, Jeremiah or one of the prophets."

"But what about you?" he asked. "Who do you say I am?"

Simon Peter answered, "You are the Messiah, the Son of the living God."

Jesus replied, "Blessed are you, Simon son of Jonah, for this was not revealed to you by flesh and blood, but by my Father in heaven." (Matthew 16:13-17/NIV)

Those were the moments when Jesus could really break things down in a relevant way that they could all understand. It was in those intimate settings when the disciples started to see the light. They didn't fully understand until after Jesus' death and resurrection. That's when it clicked. That's when they were truly ready to deliver the message that Jesus had been depositing inside their hearts.

LETTERS BETWEEN FRIENDS

After Jesus ascended into Heaven, the disciples went from being disciples (followers of Christ) to apostles (teachers of the gospel). As time passed, they began to lay the foundation for a church that has been impacting the world for more than two thousand years. Their story underscores what happens when leaders effectively communicate a core message to their team.

Now it was time for the apostles to engage in some effective internal Communication amongst themselves and amongst the early Christians. Peter and John were considered two of the most influential leaders. The group expanded with the arrival of teammates such as Matthias, Timothy, Barnabas, Apollos, and a former anti-Christian zealot named Saul who experienced the most spectacular conversion in Early Church history and changed his name to Paul.

In the early first century, there was no such thing as mass Communication in the form of telephones, radios, televisions, or the Internet, but these leaders needed to stay in touch as they traveled hundreds of miles apart. So they relied on the only form of communication available at the time—they wrote each other letters. For instance, 1 and 2 Timothy were a series of letters that Paul wrote to his young mentor.

Some of the letters were meant for a larger audience such as Romans, 1 and 2 Corinthians, Galatians, Ephesians, Philippians, Colossians, 1 and 2 Thessalonians, and Hebrews. These letters included teachings and instructions for the Christians in those cities and have provided invaluable guidance and inspiration for Christians ever since.

If the story of the Early Church had taken place in modern times, I'm sure the apostles would have broadcast their message just like we do today. But there is still something personal about handwritten messages. My wife, Connie, taught me the value of that concept. When she was either very pleased or very displeased, she would write me a letter. Sometimes they were love letters. Sometimes they were truth letters.

I wish I had done it more often during my career, but I can think of one time when writing a personal letter made a significant difference. When I was the head coach at Boston University, my nephew, Russell, was one of my players. Russell was an emotional kid, and I needed to get more out of him on the court. So I wrote him an occasional letter of encouragement. Russell always received those letters positively, and I truly believed that those acts of kindness helped spur growth and development.

However you communicate to your team, take some time to make it heartfelt and personal. Those kinds of messages (both individually and collectively) can have a lasting impact on the recipients. Just think about the impact that the New Testament letters have had on the Christian Church. It's amazing to think what can happen when you take the time to let those under your leadership know how you feel.

SEVEN KEYS TO INTERNAL COMMUNICATION (OR SPEAKING TO YOUR TEAM)

Sometimes as leaders, there's such a heavy Commitment toward a vision or a goal that it's easy to take things personally when your team members don't listen, or fail to follow through. In those moments, you can lose sight of the very people with whom you are trying to Communicate.

This is true for a new business owner, a new coach, a new parent, or even a new Christian. This is what leads many to become overzealous. The natural tendency is to want so desperately to give the people you're leading the information and the knowledge that you've received, but you have to do it the right way.

Your ability to communicate a message outside of your organization is only as good as your ability to communicate effectively to the team members inside of your organization. Here are seven keys that will help you exercise wisdom in this vitally important leadership skill:

1. Measure Your Words. Think before you speak. This isn't just important within the leadership dynamic, but within any interpersonal Communication that takes place in your life. Taking time to measure your words can help you stave off chaos and maintain a spirit of unity.

"My dear brothers and sisters, take note of this: everyone should be quick to listen, slow to speak and slow to become angry." (James 1:19/NIV)

2. Focus On The Positive. Be an encourager. Give them a reason to believe in themselves. Uplifting Communication goes miles farther than harsh criticism.

"Let your conversation be always full of grace, seasoned with salt, so that you may know how to answer everyone." (Colossians 4:6)

3. Don't Dwell On The Negative. Sometimes criticism is necessary, but it doesn't have to make the recipient walk away feeling awful about themselves. Instead, make sure criticism is constructive, sparse, and coupled with positive reinforcement.

"A gentle answer deflects anger, but harsh words make tempers flare." (Proverbs 15:1)

4. Get Everyone On The Same Page. Don't send mixed messages. In other words, don't say different things to different people. There's nothing worse for team unity than the team members not having a clear understanding of their roles and how they are expected to work together.

"Is there any encouragement from belonging to Christ? Any comfort from his love? Any fellowship together in the Spirit? Are your hearts tender and compassionate? Then make me truly happy by agreeing wholeheartedly with each other, loving one another, and working together with one mind and purpose." (Philippians 2:1-2/NLT)

5. Open The Floor. There's no way one person will have all the answers. Allow others to contribute ideas. You never know which team member might have a solution you need. And in the process, the group will become more invested in the greater vision.

"Plans fail for lack of counsel, but with many advisers they succeed." (Proverbs 15:22/NIV)

6. Observe, Ask, And Listen. Follow the example of Jesus. Understand where your team members are coming from through observation. Then, take time to ask good questions, and be willing to listen to what they have to say. You will build respect, trust, and camaraderie within the group.

"Tune your ears to wisdom, and concentrate on understanding. Cry out for insight, and ask for understanding." (Proverbs 2:2-3/NLT)

7. Put It In Writing. Have a vision plan. Make it plain for everyone to see. If you feel like things are straying from the original message, go back and look at what you have written down so you can get yourself and the team back on track.

"Then the LORD said to me, Write my answer plainly on tablets, so that a runner can carry the correct message to others.'" (Habakkuk 2:2/NLT)

STUDY QUESTIONS

1. Can you think of a time where you handled interpersonal Communication poorly while serving in a leadership role? What would you have done differently?

2. What are your strengths as an interpersonal Communicator? How have those strengths played to your advantage as a leader?

3. What are your weaknesses as an interpersonal Communicator? How have those weaknesses hindered your effectiveness as a leader?

4. What are some inspirations that you take away from reading about how Jesus Communicated with His team—the disciples?

5. How often do you ask your team members questions? How has that Communication skill made a difference in your ability to convey messages to your team?

6. Of the seven keys listed, which ones do you find most challenging? How do you think doing a better job implementing those keys might help you become a better interpersonal Communicator?

7. What are some things you can start doing today that will help you become more effective when Communicating a message (goals, visions, game plans, encouragement, correction, etc.) to your team?

FOLLOW THROUGH

• Think about what kind of message you would want your family, team, organization, church, etc., to communicate to the general public, then do one or more of the following:

• List your top three core values, which represent what you stand for.

• List three things you want to accomplish during your lifetime.

• Design a logo or crest that tells others who you are.

• Write your eulogy.

• Read through and meditate on the scriptures found throughout this chapter. If you'd like to do some additional Bible study on internal Communication, here are some verses to get you started: Habakkuk 2:2, Colossians 4:6, James 1:19.

PRAYER

Lord, give me the right words to say when speaking to those on my team. Grant me wisdom, insight, boldness, and grace as I Communicate to them the vision with which You have entrusted me. Help me be an encourager. Help me be a better listener. Help me be strong and decisive. Amen.

CHAPTER SEVEN: COMMUNICATION II
SPEAKING TO YOUR AUDIENCE

"Let everything you say be good and helpful, so that your words will be an encouragement to those who hear them."
–Ephesians 4:29b (NLT)

As the leader of any group or organization, one of your primary jobs is to communicate the core message to a target audience. That might not make sense coming from a former head coach. Most would assume that my primary jobs were as follows (and listed in order): win, win, and keep winning.

Yes, winning was important if I wanted to stay employed, but there was much more to it than that. Just like large corporations, small businesses, educational institutions, non-profit groups, and even churches, sports teams also communicate a message, which is sometimes referred to as a "brand." This is how an organization wants to be perceived or what an organization is all about. Taking that message into the public square is vitally necessary if you want to successfully complete your defined mission.

THE ART OF THE BARNSTORM

In 1956, my older brother, Richard, saved up some money and took me to my first Celtics game at the old Boston Garden. It just so happened to be the first time future Hall of Fame center Bill Russell started during his rookie season. He was one of several star players on a team that instantly captured my imagination. There were other greats like Bob Cousy, Tom Heinsohn, Frank Ramsey, and Bill Sharman. Later on, an incredible group of athletes would join the club—talented men such as K.C. Jones, Sam Jones, and Tom "Satch" Sanders.

As much as I watched the players, it was legendary head coach Red Auerbach who really captured my attention. Even as a kid, I found myself analyzing his demeanor, how he managed his players and the referees, and how he put a team together.

Many years later, I was blessed with the opportunity to meet Coach Auerbach while serving as an assistant coach with one of his former players, Tom "Satch" Sanders, at Harvard University. Years later, I would become the head coach at Red's alma mater, the George Washington University, and our friendship grew and grew. I referred to Red as my "Godfather" and he became one of my most important and valuable mentors.

Back in the 1950s and 1960s, the NBA wasn't a billion dollar industry like it is today. In fact, it was a real struggle to get fans to buy into this fledgling professional sport. Coach Auerbach had a vision that would help bring the game to prominence, and it all started with the kinds of players he would bring to Boston.

First and foremost, Coach Auerbach adhered to the advice he had once given me and that was to recruit "character not characters." Second, he looked for players with other characteristics such as discipline, competitiveness, humility, and physical conditioning. Of course, being great ball handlers, shooters, rebounders, defenders, and team players didn't hurt.

Then, Coach Auerbach took a unique approach to spreading the word about his team. He piled them into his Cadillac convertible and barnstormed all over New England where they would scrimmage and conduct free clinics. Barnstorming wasn't Red's original idea. Baseball teams did it as early as 1860 to expose more people to the game, and the Negro League athletes also barnstormed as a way of bypassing bans on blacks in the professional ranks.

It's fun to imagine Coach Auerbach behind the wheel of his caddy filled with smoke from one of his trademark victory cigars— although by most accounts, some of those rides weren't too much fun for the players thanks to his notoriously poor driving habits. Somehow, they always managed to get to their destinations safely. It might have been a youth clinic at a YMCA in Worchester or an exhibition at a high school gym in Cape Cod. Red wasn't out to save the world. He was just selling the Celtics and the NBA.

And because of the small venues, people got an up-close look at these talented and fundamentally sound ballplayers who also happened to be well mannered, well-dressed, well-educated, and spoke proper English. If you saw them in the airports, they would be reading books, or *The New York Times*, or *The Wall Street Journal*. They were very image conscious. They were considerate and polite. That's the visual message Red wanted to send, and the more he could share that message, the more fans he could attract to the games— especially families with young kids.

It didn't take long for Coach Auerbach's plan to bear fruit. The Boston Garden started to fill up, and the club paid the people back with some excellent basketball. During Red's tenure as the head coach, the Celtics won nine championships and another seven titles under his leadership as General Manager.

When I first took over at Cambridge Rindge and Latin, I wanted to communicate a similar message. I modeled the high school program's brand after what Coach Auerbach did with the Celtics. The student body, the faculty, the community, and any outsiders looking in were going to see what a team should look like.

We had great players like Patrick Ewing and Rumeal Robinson, but no one player would be totally responsible for our success. Our brand on the court was balanced scoring and great defense. Our brand off the court was equally important. The Warriors would be well respected as student-athletes and Cambridge citizens.

That was our brand, and my job as the leader (just like I learned from Coach Auerbach) was to communicate that message in both word and in deed. And in many ways, it was just as important as winning games and state championship trophies.

THE GREATEST STORYTELLER EVER

Just like most of us, I have my fair share of regrets. Too often I ponder the question, "What if?" Thankfully those thoughts don't last long. I only have one chance to live, and I can't go back in time and take a mulligan. That's why I tell stories. It's my way of paying it forward and imparting some hard-earned wisdom along the way.

As I embark on this portion of the journey, my greatest inspiration is Jesus of Nazareth. He was the greatest communicator to walk the earth. Nobody could get a point across better than Him, and so many times He used stories (or parables), metaphors, and sermons to share the message. We can learn a lot about external Communication from His example:

1. His stories were <u>culturally relevant</u>. Many of the main characters were shepherds and farmers, common professions of that day. He also talked about the socioeconomic gap between the poor and the rich—something of which everyone was keenly aware. Jesus even tackled racial and religious issues, for instance, in the iconic story of the Good Samaritan (Luke 10:25-42)—a man who

was considered a lower class citizen yet helped a Jewish man in need when two religious leaders refused to get their hands dirty—and in the process, shared a timeless message about what it means to love your neighbor.

2. Jesus' parables were <u>simple</u>. He didn't need to tell a long, drawn out story to make a point, and yet His memorable parables (some as short as two sentences) have stood the test of time and are continuing to make an impact on the world over two thousand years later. That was part of the plan: tell simple but powerful stories that can be easily passed along from generation to generation.

3. No matter the method, Jesus' message was always <u>pointed</u>. He knew exactly to whom He was speaking and exactly what they needed to hear. Jesus knew it was controversial for a Jewish man to speak to a Samaritan woman. He did it anyway. Jesus knew how the religious leaders would react to His teachings. He boldly shared them anyway. Jesus also knew that there were many poor and desperate people who needed to hear His message of redemption and hope. He shared it willingly, even though it eventually led him to His death on the Cross.

4. Most importantly, Jesus was <u>consistent</u>. He stayed on message. Whether He was telling a story or conveying a spiritual truth, it was always about the Kingdom of God (or, as He often called it, the Kingdom of Heaven). That way, there could ultimately be no question of motivation or intent. Everything He said was meant to draw people closer to Him, so He could transform their hearts and change their lives.

Sometimes I wonder why we bother studying anyone else. In my mind, Jesus will always be the greatest communicator that our world's history has ever recorded. I pray for even a fraction of His insight and skill as an orator of the Good News.

A SIMPLE, RELEVANT GOSPEL

When Jesus ascended into Heaven, it didn't take long for the disciples to realize that they had some huge shoes to fill. They had spent three and a half years listening to the Master Communicator share the Good News at a broad level to the masses, while at the same time learning its intricacies behind the scenes. Still, they must have felt overwhelmingly inadequate to carry on in His name.

Of course, we know that God sent them the Holy Spirit as their comforter and guide. They received boldness to share the message in hostile environments while edifying each other through private meetings and detailed letters. To no one's surprise, they employed many of the same teaching methods that they learned from Jesus.

Atop that list was simplicity. When speaking to large groups of people, it was all about the Messiah and how His death and resurrection ushered in forgiveness of sin and the promise of eternal life. All throughout the Book of Acts, they proclaimed the message. They were bold. They were unwavering. They were to the point.

And then came a man named Paul.

The apostle Paul wasn't one of the original disciples. In fact, he was a Jewish zealot with Roman citizenship who made it his personal mission to kill or imprison as many Christians as possible. Originally known as Saul, his life was radically changed when he had a miraculous encounter with Jesus, which can be read in Acts 9.

Throughout his subsequent ministry, Paul found himself in some unusual places and speaking to some unlikely groups of people. In Athens, he debated philosophers and shared the gospel with pagans. In Jerusalem, he catered his message toward the Jews who had not yet accepted the divine nature of Christ. Paul even spoke in Aramaic to gain credibility with the most conservative among them. In Rome, he took advantage of his Roman citizenship to argue for his physical freedom, while at the same time preaching a message of spiritual freedom. In one of his letters to the church in Corinth, he explained the reason behind this method of Communication:

"Though I am free and belong to no one, I have made myself a slave to everyone, to win as many as possible. To the Jews I became like a Jew, to win the Jews. To those under the law I became like one under the law (though I myself am not under the law), so as to win those under the law. To those not having the law I became like one not having the law (though I am not free from God's law but am under Christ's law), so as to win those not having the law. To the weak I became weak, to win the weak. I have become all things to all people so that by all possible means I might save some. I do all this for the sake of the gospel, that I may share in its blessings." – 1 Corinthians 9:19-23 (NIV)

Reading about Paul and the apostles' approach has challenged me to be more thoughtful in how I communicate with the different audiences to whom I speak. Most of my life, that Communication has been to the athletes on my teams, but more recently I've been blessed with the opportunity to speak to churches, men's groups, school children, business leaders, married couples, educators, inmates, and police officers. Keeping it simple and relevant continues to be one of my primary goals every time I share my story.

SEVEN KEYS TO EXTERNAL COMMUNICATION (OR SPEAKING TO YOUR AUDIENCE)

It doesn't matter if your message is something as nuanced as a brand (like Red Auerbach and his Boston Celtics) or something that's much more direct (like the gospel message of Christ and His disciples). Figuring out your message (as discussed in chapter six) only matters if you can effectively take that message beyond the four walls of your organization. With that in mind, here are seven keys to external Communication or, more simply put, speaking to your audience.

1. Know Your Audience. Be relevant. Like Jesus did during His ministry, use culturally appropriate stories and analogies that your target group will understand and appreciate. When necessary, change the delivery of your message (but never the message itself) in an effort to relate to whomever you are addressing.

"I have become all things to all people so that by all possible means I might save some." (1 Corinthians 9:22b/NIV)

2. Be Prepared. Practice what you preach—in the literal sense. Don't wing it. Whether it's sharing your organization's core message or sharing your faith, you should never be caught off guard when someone wants to know more or has questions. Rehearse what you might say in a variety of scenarios that include both positive and negative confrontations.

"And if someone asks about your hope as a believer, always be ready to explain it." – 1 Peter 3:15b (NLT)

3. Keep It Simple. Too many messages at once will only confuse your audience and sometimes can confuse yourself. Simplicity is the key to being a good leader. Communicating ideas and concepts should become as natural as breathing.

"A truly wise person uses few words; a person with understanding is even-tempered." (Proverbs 17:27/NLT)

4. Be Bold. Your message might not always be popular or politically correct, but share it with confidence and courage. At the same time, do so in the most non-abrasive manner possible. People will be more apt to listen when they are approached with genuine compassion and care.

"Instead, we will speak the truth in love, growing in every way more and more like Christ, who is the head of his body, the church." (Ephesians 4:15/NLT)

5. Stay On Message. Too much talk can get you in trouble. When you've made your point, there's no need to keep going. It often doesn't end well. Instead, be disciplined in your Communication, and leave the door open for an invitation back. Present your message in a way that will make people want to hear more.

"Avoid worthless, foolish talk that only leads to more godless behavior." (2 Timothy 2:16/NLT)

6. Make It Memorable. You might have only one shot to communicate your message, so take a creative and skillful approach. Frame things in a way that makes your message easy to remember. Use acronyms, alliteration, and other forms of repetition. It also helps to have props and video presentations if possible.

So often, words blow into the wind, but if people can visualize the message, it's easier for them to recall your key talking points. And when doing so, speak to their heart and draw them into your story.

"Do you see a man skillful in his work? He will stand before kings; he will not stand before obscure men." (Proverbs 22:29/ESV)

7. Refine The Message. Communication is an ongoing process. If at any point you begin to lose effectiveness, consider new strategies so you can rethink your delivery or streamline the message. This doesn't mean you change the message, but you may need to trim the fat and eliminate any parts that don't advance the cause.

"From a wise mind comes wise speech; the words of the wise are persuasive." (Proverbs 16:23/NLT)

STUDY QUESTIONS

1. On a scale of one to ten, how would you rank the importance of Communication when it comes to conveying your organization's message to the outside public or targeted audience? Explain.

2. What are some challenges that you have personally faced when trying to externally Communicate your message? Were you able to devise any solutions? If so, what worked for you?

3. Is it possible to effectively Communicate your message without knowing and understanding the audience? Explain.

4. Can you describe a time when your message became overcomplicated? What problems did that cause, and what did you do to simplify the message?

5. What does the word "cultural relevance" mean to you? What are some ways that you have tried to craft your message in a culturally relevant way?

6. Of the seven keys to speaking to an audience, which ones have you found most helpful in your Communication efforts? Which ones have you found most challenging?

7. What are some things you can start to do today that will help you become more effective in Communicating your message to your target audience?

FOLLOW THROUGH

• Call someone you haven't talked to in a while, and ask them about their life and how they're doing.

• Record a new voice message on your phone that is positive, encouraging, and uplifting.

• Find and listen to a Christian radio station, like Moody Radio, and listen to it on your way to and from work.

• Craft a single sentence that you can use to tell others who you are.

• Read through and meditate on the scriptures found throughout this chapter. If you'd like to do some additional Bible study on external Communication, here are some verses to get you started: Proverbs 16:23, Ephesians 4:15, Ephesians 4:29.

PRAYER

Lord, I want to be a strong Communicator of the message of Your truth. Help me use wisdom as I boldly and courageously share the words that You have given me. Help me better understand my audience, and give me creativity to effectively use my platform. It's all for Your glory. Amen.

CHAPTER EIGHT: COMMUNITY I
STRENGTHENING THE FAMILY

"Though one may be overpowered, two can defend themselves. A cord of three strands is not quickly broken."
–Ecclesiastes 4:12 (NIV)

In chapters nine and ten, we'll be discussing the importance of fostering <u>internal</u> Community (through personal and organizational accountability) and the responsibility of actively serving others in the <u>external</u> Community.

Real Community, however, starts in the home. Family is the foundation for Community. It's where leadership should be bred, born, and grown, and in many ways, it's a growing lack of moral direction in the home that has led to a leadership vacuum in our nation.

So before we go any further, let's first take a closer look at the most important building block for Community—the family.

CONNIE'S STORY

My wife, Connie, is very passionate about marriage and the family. Because of where we are in our culture, people aren't clear on what marriage is supposed to look like and what it's supposed to be about. I share that same passion, and our goal, as a married couple of more than fifty years, is to teach others what God had in mind when He created marriage.

First, however, it will help to have a better understanding of Connie's background and why this topic is so dear to her heart. This is her story in her own words:

My mother came from Barbados when she was 17 years old. She came through Ellis Island to live with her uncle in New York. My mom got married in her mid-20s and had seven children. My dad, however, died when I was two years old, leaving me without a father figure during my early years. It remained that way until she remarried a strong, Christian man from our church named Joseph Hurley that we called "Dads."

My mom worked unbelievably hard to keep everybody together. Because she worked so hard, I didn't really have a close relationship with her—the kind you would expect the youngest child to have with their mother. I know that she loved us even though she wasn't the most demonstrative person, but her Commitment to provide for her family spoke for itself.

While mom was busy putting clothes on our backs, a roof over our heads, and food on the table, I looked to my siblings for direction. I did a lot of observing. I watched how they behaved and took note of what was good and what wasn't so good. I tried to emulate what was good and stay away from what wasn't good.

Ultimately, it was my mother's example that taught me about leadership. She was one of the matriarchs of the church. She was a very strong Christian woman who had high, moral character and deep faith. She worked very hard in the church and in the community as well. My mom was very generous. Even though she didn't have a lot, she was willing to share whatever she could—not to get anything back, but because she was trying to be the hands of Jesus.

Despite the challenges, my mom accomplished so much in her life. She wasn't a high school graduate, but if you ever heard her speak, you would have thought she went to Harvard. She was unbelievable. She spoke many times at church and prayed in front of large groups. She was also an incredible businesswoman. She was one of the biggest real estate owners in Cambridge. She was highly skilled and very bright.

It was my mother's Character traits, however, that impacted me the most and helped me become the person I am today. Those were the traits that I tried to emulate as a young person and have continued to pursue throughout my entire life. I can say with all truthfulness that my mom taught me everything I needed to know about being a leader—as a wife, as a mother, as a community servant, and as a member of the Body of Christ.

Connie and I had a lot in common. Although we didn't have strong father figures, we were blessed to learn about leadership from our moms as well as our siblings and strong leaders in the Community (pastors, teachers, coaches, etc.). Only by the grace of God did we come together as teenage friends turned high school sweethearts, turned husband and wife.

I first remember seeing her the summer before my ninth grade year when our family moved into the house next door. Connie has an earlier memory of me that I have conveniently forgotten:

I was about eight years old, and every Saturday everybody in the neighborhood would go to the movie theater. I would be sitting with my friends and all of the sudden this little, chubby kid in a white t-shirt and husky jeans would come running through the theater, terrorizing all the girls. Can you imagine?

Thankfully, I made a much better impression in the weeks following our family's move from Howard Street to River Street. Every Sunday morning Connie would go to church with her mother and her sisters. As she was getting ready, she would notice me walking to church by myself. She would later tell me that it was one of the things she admired most—that I would willingly go to church even though I didn't have to go.

Connie and I began dating in high school and got married in our early 20s. By then, my coaching career was already in motion. I was an assistant at Northeastern and Harvard before taking the job at my high school alma mater, Cambridge Rindge & Latin, where we won three consecutive state championships. I then took my first college head coach position at Boston University.

During that time, Connie went back to school where she earned a Master of Arts degree in Education and Human Development from Emmanuel College in Boston. She was also working and raising the kids. There was no way I could have been successful without her.

Toward the end of my time at Boston University, Connie was accepted into the prestigious School of Social Work there. That's when I was offered the job at The George Washington University in D.C. It was one of the hardest things for her to do, but she walked away from that opportunity and made the decision that she would set her goals aside and get even more actively involved in my career.

Connie traveled with the team. She was the mother, the big sister, and the aunt to the players. She invited them into our home for meals, took care of them when they were sick, and counseled them when they needed some motherly love and wisdom. It was her goal to expose them to different career options and help them network with the academic and alumni communities. She understood that they needed to start thinking about what happens with the rest of their lives.

It was a sacrifice, but she gained from the experience. More importantly, it was the two of us working together for a common goal—to prepare our players for life after basketball in the workplace and the home. We wanted our marriage to be an example to them and to serve as an encouragement for what they could enjoy in their future as husbands and fathers.

THE DINNER TABLE

It shouldn't surprise anyone that the Jarvis household approached daily life as a team. Each person had a role. We always worked together no matter what we were doing. Connie and I modeled the team concept from the beginning and that continued as our son, Mike Jr., and daughter, Dana, along with our two foster girls, Angelique and Frances, got older and gained more responsibilities.

From a parenting standpoint, it was vitally important that we were always on the same page. Our daughter, Dana, for instance, might ask me for something and I would say, "No." Like kids often do, however, she would go to her mom and ask the same thing. The answer was still, "No." We had a policy that whatever one of us said, the other would agree. Our kids couldn't break down the team.

Communication was one of the most important aspects within our family, and some of our best communication took place around the dinner table. That was the meeting place. That was the place where people reviewed their day and talked about what was on their mind, shared whatever problems they might've had, and asked for assistance when needed.

Connie was famous for calling for family meetings. When things needed to be discussed, we would discuss them as a family. If there was an issue or a problem, we wanted to deal with it once and put the cards on the table. We were going to deal with it as a family. We were going to have a family discussion and we would say what we had to say. Connie always asked good questions. From there, we would listen to what the kids had to say.

When we eat dinner, even if it's just the two of us, there's no phone or television. We did that with our kids and our teams because it's one of the best times for a good conversation. Every meal started with a prayer and thanksgiving. Last, but not least, it helped that Connie was a great cook.

We believed that the dinner table was the great meeting place for the family. It gave everybody an opportunity to talk to one another and have important discussions. Some of the most important times in the history of mankind have involved food and conversation—like the Lord's Supper when Jesus shared some deep and meaningful revelations with His disciples.

Unfortunately, families in today's culture don't do that nearly enough. Now, you go to a restaurant, and you see the kids (and the parents) on their phones or tablets. They have everything to keep them occupied. The one thing they don't have is conversation. We would be so much stronger in our relationships if we could get back to a place of open and honest communication with the family.

If your family is struggling with this, try making a concerted effort to reclaim the dinner table as a starting point to strengthening the relationships within your home. It's never too late to get back to the basics and foster stronger Community.

THE FIRST FAMILY

Marriage is a principal building block of our society. It's possible to make such a definitive statement because the Bible clearly shows us how important it was for a man and a woman to come together as husband and wife.

God's plan was revealed in Genesis 2 where He saw that Adam, the first man created, needed a companion:

So the LORD God caused the man to fall into a deep sleep; and while he was sleeping, he took one of the man's ribs and then closed up the place with flesh. Then the LORD God made a woman from the rib he had taken out of the man, and he brought her to the man.

> *The man said,*
> *"This is now bone of my bone*
> *and flesh of my flesh;*
> *she shall be called 'woman,'*
> *for she was taken out of man."*
> *That is why a man leaves his father and mother and is united*
to his wife, and they become one flesh. (vv. 21-24/NIV)

God's plan for marriage didn't stop there. He instructed Adam and Eve to "be fruitful and increase in number" (Genesis 1:28/NIV). God used them to introduce the concept of family, which in turn served as the foundation for the larger community.

Family is the key to thriving societies and cultures. It's no wonder that Satan attacked it from the very beginning. In Genesis 3, we read the tragic story of how Satan tempted Adam and Eve to disobey God and how that introduced sin into the world and caused man's fellowship with Him to be broken.

Satan then caused strife between mankind's first brothers—Cain and Abel—which led to history's first recorded murder. Since then, his relentless assault on the family has continued nonstop. Men began to marry multiple wives. Siblings began to fight against each other for familial control.

Those are storylines that can be readily found in just the first few books of the Old Testament. Even in the last fifty plus years, however, we've witnessed the tragic increase of divorce, an alarming number of children born without two parents, and the redefinition of marriage that goes outside of God's original plan.

As leaders within the home, it is our responsibility to model biblical marriage so that our children and others in our circle of influence will see what God intended for the family. When we are invited to a wedding, Connie has something special she likes to give the newlywed couple. It's a card with a poem called "Cord of Three Strands," which also includes an actual cord. The purple strand represents the groom. The white strand represents the bride. The gold strand in the middle represents God. At the bottom of the card is a poignant verse that ties it all together:

Though one may be overpowered, two can defend themselves. A cord of three strands is not quickly broken. (Ecclesiastes 4:12/NIV)

God put Connie and I together, and it's only by God's grace that we are still here today, some fifty years later. The same is true for the married people reading this book, and it will also hold true for any single people who hope to be married in the future. The key to it all, however, is putting God in the center. That's the only way a marriage and a family will truly stand the test of time.

FAMILY MATTERS

God could have sent Jesus to earth in many different ways. He could have sent His Son as a mighty warrior. He could have sent Jesus as a mysterious prophet. He could have sent Him as a heavenly creature. No one, however, expected God to send Him as a newborn baby.

Theologians have pondered the reason why Jesus came as a child for centuries. Many have theorized that it was to show Him as fully human so he could experience life just like anyone else. There were also many prophecies that needed to be fulfilled, and Jesus' lowly beginning certainly assured that the Hebrew Scriptures would come to pass.

In essence, God was introducing the second Adam—a man who would live a perfect, sinless life and eventually become the sacrifice for our sins. Jesus came into the world as part of a family unit. His arrival was a powerful reminder of God's original plan. God also used two ordinary people (Mary and Joseph) and put them through an extraordinary circumstance that ushered in the greatest miracle mankind has ever witnessed—the virgin birth.

Jesus' arrival was also the culmination of Adam's lineage as it made its way through an unlikely cast of characters. He used a liar (Abraham), a deceiver (Jacob), a prostitute (Rahab), a widow (Ruth), an adulterer (David), a philanderer (Solomon), and many other imperfect people to bring this divine family together.

It should come as no surprise that Jesus, and later His disciples (who became known as apostles), had a lot to say about family matters. Here are a few key points:

• Marriage is a lifelong Commitment (Matthew 19:6).

• Husbands and wives should respectfully submit to each other (Ephesians 5:21).

• The husband is the head of the home (Ephesians 5:23).

• Husbands are to lead with love (Ephesians 5:25-30; Colossians 3:19).

• Wives are to submit with respect (Ephesians 5:22-24; Colossians 3:18).

• Parents should teach their children in the ways of the Lord (Ephesians 6:4).

• Parents should discipline their children with love (Hebrews 12:11).

• Parents should not provoke their children (Colossians 3:21).

• Parents should provide for their families (1 Timothy 5:8).

Connie and I would never claim to have been perfect spouses or perfect parents, but throughout our marriage we have done our very best to live out these biblical teachings. Our prayer was to teach our children about God's plan for the family.

We have been blessed to see them both follow in our footsteps as they have also tried to be godly spouses and parents. They have also become not only leaders in their homes, but also leaders in the Community, in the church, and in their places of work.

As you prepare for marriage or work toward strengthening your existing marriage, never forget that true biblical leadership begins at home. It is our responsibility as husbands, wives, and children to learn all we can within the home before stepping out and becoming the leaders that God has called us to be outside of the home.

SEVEN KEYS TO STRENGTHENING THE FAMILY

Some of you might be thinking it's too late to strengthen your family. Past mistakes and hurts may have left your home fractured or left for dead. Jesus says differently. There is always time to return to His original plan for your family.

Whether you are already deep into your life as a spouse and/or parent, or you have yet to step into that lifelong commitment, here are seven keys to strengthening the family and laying the groundwork for stronger communities:

1. Put God In The Center. This is the first and only step that will truly allow your marriage and your family to be strong and able to endure the tests that will surely come your way.

"Though one may be overpowered, two can defend themselves. A cord of three strands is not quickly broken." (Ecclesiastes 4:12/NIV)

2. Seek Wise Counsel. Before you get married, go through biblically based pre-marital counseling so you can fully understand the purpose, function, and expectations of marriage. Don't stop there. Continue to grow in your relationship through small groups and by seeking out mentoring from seasoned, godly married couples.

"Get all the advice and instruction you can, so you will be wise the rest of your life." (Proverbs 19:20/NLT)

3. Get On The Same Page. Communicate regularly about what you want to see in your marriage. Have a unified vision for yourselves and for your children. Take these things to God in prayer. Then, in your parenting, be consistent on matters such as discipline and spiritual training.

"Then make me truly happy by agreeing wholeheartedly with each other, loving one another, and working together with one mind and purpose." (Philippians 2:2/NLT)

4. Be Alert. Satan hates the family and seeks to destroy it at every turn. Be aware of his schemes, and protect your family from his attacks through prayer, Bible devotion, and through regular Communication with your spouse and children about spiritual matters.

"Stay alert! Watch out for your great enemy, the devil. He prowls around like a roaring lion, looking for someone to devour." (1 Peter 5:8/NLT)

5. Make Time For Quality Time. Don't be too busy or caught up in everyday life. Be intentional in creating opportunities for conversation, prayer time, Bible devotion, and family fun. Talk over meals about important issues. Educate your children about what's going on in the world. Use those moments to teach a biblical worldview that will lead them down the path of righteousness.

"Slow down. Take a deep breath. What's the hurry? Why wear yourself out? Just what are you after anyway?" (Jeremiah 2:25a/MSG)

6. Lead By Example. Be the parent. Don't try to be your child's best friend. Lack of maturity sets a bad example. Assume the role of teacher. It's your job to show them not only biblical truths but also life skills through your words *and* through your actions.

"Be shepherds of God's flock that is under your care, watching over them—not because you must, but because you are willing, as God wants you to be; not pursuing dishonest gain, but eager to serve; not lording it over those entrusted to you, but being examples to the flock." (1 Peter 5:2-3/NIV)

7. Serve God Together. Don't just attend church together, but serve in your church together. Participate in small groups as a family. Get involved in the Community. It's important to actively show your children what it looks like to be a servant leader and to do so with your love for God as the motivation.

"But as for me and my family, we will serve the LORD." (Joshua 24:15b/NLT)

STUDY QUESTIONS

1. From your personal experience, how would you define the word "family?" Does that word generally bring back positive memories or negative memories? Explain.

2. Who in your family (immediate or extended) were the people that taught you the most about leadership? How have you applied those lessons throughout your life?

3. What do you think is the significance of the story of Adam and Eve (why God created Eve, why He told them to "be fruitful," etc.)?

4. What do you think is the most important reason why God chose to send Jesus to earth as a baby and through an ordinary couple like Mary and Joseph? What does the lineage of Christ say about the kind of people God is willing to use?

5. Go back and look at the list of New Testament teachings on marriage and family. Which ones do you think modern society tends to struggle with most, and how has that negatively impacted our communities today?

6. What do you think it should look like to "put God in the center" of your marriage and your family? How might that help make your marriage and your family stronger?

7. Of the other six keys listed, which ones do you find most challenging to live out? What are some specific ways that consistently doing those things might improve your home life?

FOLLOW THROUGH

• Start every meal by giving thanks to God. Alternate that privilege with other members in your group or family.

• Institute a no-electronics policy at the dinner table.

• Use dinner time to hold a family meeting where you can talk about the day's activities and important issues (faith, culture, current events, the future, etc.).

• Create a weekly schedule to spend individual time with each of your children to have fun and to talk about important issues (faith, culture, the future, etc.).

• Create a calendar of events to ensure that you know what your spouse and children are doing throughout the month.

• Read through and meditate on the scriptures found throughout this chapter. If you'd like to do some additional Bible study on Community within the family, here are some verses to get you started: Joshua 24:15, Ecclesiastes 4:12, 1 Peter 5:2-3.

PRAYER

Lord, I want to be the leader in my home that You have called me to be. Help me put You in the center of my family relationships. Give me the courage to seek wise counsel. Bring unity into my home. Help me be more consistent as I try to lead by example. Make me aware of the enemy's schemes against me and my loved ones. Bring us together as we share quality time in prayer and in Your Word, and as we serve You in unity. Amen.

CHAPTER NINE: COMMUNITY II
BEING HELD ACCOUNTABLE

"Iron sharpens iron; so a man sharpens a friend's character."
–Ecclesiastes 4:9 (ISV)

Stepping outside of the family unit (the first and most important example of Community), there are two other kinds of Community—the kind that takes place within an organization and the kind that takes place outside the four walls of that organization. In chapter ten, we'll discuss what it looks like to model servant leadership and have an impact on the external Community. But first, it's vitally important that you (as an individual) and your team (as a group) are engaged in consistently meaningful and honest modes of accountability.

TRUSTED VOICES

In 1973, I was hired as an assistant at Harvard University. I spent the next four years working closely with head coach and former Celtics great, Tom "Satch" Sanders. One of my primary responsibilities was to be his inner voice—someone he could trust to make suggestions on a variety of issues. Satch was always going to make the final decision, but I still needed to be confident and speak the truth. Sometimes that meant telling him things he didn't want to hear or things that weren't comfortable to discuss.

During one season, we had a player who wasn't about the team. One night after a tough loss, I called him out in front of the team, questioning his attitude and Commitment to our success. His disrespectful response made matters worse. In fact, things got so bad that I asked him to turn in his uniform and leave the locker room. He was our tallest and most talented player, but no one was more important than the team. I was certain that Satch would agree with my decision, and I was right. Satch backed me one hundred percent. He never questioned my decision and said he would have done the same thing. I'll never forget the trust and faith he had in me.

Twenty years after my first season at Harvard, I was the head coach at George Washington University. My son, Mike Jr., had just graduated from Boston University and told me how much he wanted to coach with me. After negotiating with his agent, who happened to be his mother, I hired Mike, and we became the first African American father-son coaching team in the history of NCAA Division I college basketball.

Twenty-one years and hundreds of wins later, we would coach our last game together in a first round loss to Marshall at the Conference USA Tournament in El Paso, Texas. For all those years, I worked side by side with my son, knowing he had my back and that he would always give me his best.

Mike was going to not only support me, but he was also going to be honest with me. He would tell me things that none of the other assistants would, even when I may not have wanted to hear it. As I look back, I wish I had invited Mike into the room more often when I was about to have a confrontational meeting with somebody I didn't like or respect. It's taken a little time away from our coaching days to realize just how much I valued him and the role he played in my life and my coaching career.

With Satch Sanders, I was the trusted voice that helped him make wise decisions. With my son, Mike Jr., he was the trusted voice that I likewise needed. In both cases, it was all about being open to the process of accountability—providing it for someone or being open to receiving it from someone. It's impossible to be a trustworthy leader without it.

A KING'S DOWNFALL

The Bible is full of some of the most powerful leaders to walk the earth. The Old Testament in particular is rich with examples of great men and women who followed God and accomplished incredible things. King David ranks near the top of that list. However, as good as David was, he made a lot of mistakes, and in some ways, he tarnished his legacy.

David's story is legendary. He killed lions and bears with his bare hands while defending his father's sheep. He then rose to fame after defeating and killing the Philistine giant, Goliath. After King Saul was killed in battle, David was appointed as the King of Judah.

Even before he was king, David surrounded himself with the best warriors. He also had wise counsel in his midst and a trusted friend and accountability partner in Jonathan, King Saul's son. But there's something that often happens when leaders reach certain levels of authority. If leaders aren't careful, they will allow things like pride, power, and success to get them off track and set aside their protections.

That's what happened to David. Even though he had counselors and spiritual guides, he didn't always let them in and he wasn't always honest with them. That led to one of the biggest mistakes of David's life—Bathsheba.

In this story, David spied on a beautiful woman who was bathing, and desired to have her for his own. There was a problem with that plan. Bathsheba was married to Uriah who just happened to be one of David's greatest military leaders. That didn't deter David from sleeping with Bathsheba who later discovered that she was pregnant with the king's child. This led David to put a plan in place that would put Uriah in harm's way on the battlefield. After Uriah's death, David married Bathsheba to complete the devious cover up.

The secret didn't stay hidden for long. God revealed David's sin to the prophet Nathan who went to the temple and called him out. David repented and was forgiven, but he still had to pay a heavy price. His and Bathsheba's child died at birth. Another son, Absalom, rebelled against him and was killed. Years later, another son, Solomon, ascended to the throne and accomplished great things, but struggled throughout his reign because of the generational curse that David passed down.

To David's credit, he always made things right. Once his failures were made public, he was open to renewed accountability and correction. But think about how much greater David's legacy would have been without those lapses in his moral judgment.

In many ways, I can relate to David as I look back and see the mistakes that I made, because I didn't always listen to my accountability partners, including my closest confidante, my wife, Connie. On the flipside, I know without a doubt that my best decisions came after listening to wise counsel and trusting the voices that God has placed in my life.

Yes, we've got to talk to God. We've got to pray and commune with Him on a daily basis. The Holy Spirit is our number one accountability partner. But here on this side of Heaven, we also need to talk to our spouses, our parents, our trusted friends, our pastoral figures, and anyone else who will help us make unselfish choices that honor God and keep us on the right path.

A HIGHER AUTHORITY

We are all accountable to someone. That's just a fact of life. Whether we choose to walk in that accountability is a completely different issue, and which direction we go will have a huge impact on our lives.

But what about Jesus? To whom was He accountable? It's a strange thought. After all, Jesus was without sin and lived a perfect life. Why would He need to submit to someone else's authority and counsel?

Well, Jesus, in fact, was accountable to someone. He was accountable to God the Father. We know this because it was something He told His disciples throughout the gospels. For instance, in John 6:38, Jesus said, *"For I have come down from heaven to do the will of God who sent me, not to do my own will." (NLT)*

And later, He responded to an inquiry from Philip this way: *"Don't you believe that I am in the Father, and that the Father is in me? The words I say to you I do not speak on my authority. Rather, it is the Father, living in me, who is doing his work." (John 14:10/NIV)*

Jesus also interjected the concept of accountability into His teachings when talking about Communication: *"And I tell you this, you must give an account on judgment day for every idle word you speak. The words you say will either acquit you or condemn you." (Matthew 12:36-37/NLT)*

And when talking about relationships: *"So watch yourselves. If your brother or sister sins against you, rebuke them; and if they repent, forgive them." (Luke 17:3/NIV)*

Jesus took it one step further when He demonstrated the true meaning of accountability and showed us what it really looks like to submit to a higher authority. This took place a few hours before His disciple Judas betrayed Him and turned Him over to the authorities. Jesus knelt and entered into a time of intense prayer.

"Father, if you are willing, take this cup from me; yet not my will, but yours be done." (Luke 22:42/NIV)

Even in Jesus' darkest hour—in a time when He could have walked away from the intense pain He was about to face—He stayed accountable to God and never wavered from the plan for His life. And that's the model for us as Christian leaders. We will always have people on earth to whom we are accountable, but none greater than the Father Himself.

SHARING THE LOAD

Just like everything the disciples learned from Jesus, the concept of accountability didn't fully click until He was gone. In Acts 2, we read about how the Early Church was born, and there's an amazing picture of what happens when leaders become accountable to each other and develop a strong sense of Community.

"All the believers devoted themselves to the apostles' teaching, and to fellowship, and to sharing in meals (including the Lord's Supper), and to prayer...And all the believers met together in one place and shared everything they had." (Acts 2:42, 43/NLT)

There are two things to point out in those verses: 1) The new Christians submitted themselves to the authority of those in charge, and 2) They spent a lot of time together. That's how their Community grew from the inside and continued to expand as people saw God's model of teamwork and accountability in action.

While the book of Acts shows us how it's done, the rest of the New Testament teaches us why it's done that way and gives us additional teaching that we should still apply to our leadership today. The apostles Peter and Paul, in particular, write about the concept of internal Community and accountability throughout their letters, and they cover the topic from the leader's and the team member's perspective.

For instance, the apostle Peter speaks to leaders about their responsibility over those under their authority: *"Be shepherds of God's flock that is under your care, watching over them—not because you must, but because you are willing, as God wants you to be; not pursuing dishonest gain, but eager to serve; not lording it over those entrusted to you, but being examples to the flock." (1 Peter 5:2-3/NIV)*

In that same passage, he turns to the other part of the equation and explains what accountability looks like from the follower's point of view: *"In the same way, you who are younger, submit yourselves to your elders. All of you clothe yourselves with humility toward one another, because 'God opposes the proud but shows favor to the humble.'" (I Peter 5:5/NIV)*

And finally, there's a third part of internal Community that is often overlooked yet equally important—this idea of getting along, working together, and sharing the load—something that the apostle Paul encourages in one of his letters to the Christians in

Thessalonica: *"Therefore encourage one another and build each other up, just as in fact you are doing." (1 Thessalonians 5:11/NIV)*

It's a beautiful thing when a leader is following God's authority and when the rest of the team is following that leader's authority. It's also a picture of the gospel. When this model of accountability is in place, things operate more smoothly. People are more effective and efficient within their roles and responsibilities. The entire organization is an enjoyable place to be.

On the flip side, when a leader is doing his or her own thing, or when the team refuses to follow the leader's authority, there's almost certainly going to be chaos, dissension, and trouble. When that occurs, people become ineffective and inefficient in their roles and responsibilities, and the entire organization is destined for failure.

No matter where you are at on the chain of authority, it's up to you to decide if you are going to be part of the problem or part of the solution.

SEVEN KEYS TO INTERNAL COMMUNITY (OR BEING HELD ACCOUNTABLE)

In this chapter, we've talked about internal Community from four different perspectives: 1) The leader's responsibility to be accountable to a higher authority, 2) The leader's responsibility to be the accountability for his or her team, 3) The team's responsibility to submit to that authority, and 4) The team's responsibility to keep each other accountable through fellowship and encouragement.

Here are seven keys that will help foster that kind of environment within your team or organization:

1. Lead By Example. You can't expect your team members to hold each other accountable if you haven't shown them what accountability looks like. Model what it looks like to submit to God's authority, and be actively involved in your own accountability relationships with your spouse, your peers, and your church. Otherwise, you will be viewed as a hypocrite, and your leadership will be undermined.

"Show proper respect to everyone, love the family of believers, fear God, honor the emperor." – 1 Peter 2:17 (NIV)

2. Create Partnerships. Set up a system where employees, team members, etc., can buddy up. Assigning older, more experienced people with younger people is especially effective.

"Iron sharpens iron; so a man sharpens a friend's character." – Ecclesiastes 4:9 (ISV)

3. Set Guidelines. Create written and verbal contracts that are based on the truth of God's Word. Make sure everyone understands the terms and agrees to abide by them. When there is any question about a rule or a regulation, you can always go back to that document as the standard to which everyone is expected to perform. That sets the tone for the process of accountability on both sides.

"All Scripture is God-breathed and is useful for teaching, rebuking, correcting, and training in righteousness, so that the servant of God may be thoroughly equipped for every good work." – 2 Timothy 3:16-17 (NIV)

4. Know The Consequences. There's no point in having guidelines if there are no real consequences attached. Be fair, be realistic, and most importantly, be consistent. Then, when the time comes, don't be afraid to correct.

"No discipline seems pleasant at the time, but painful. Later on, however, it produces a harvest of righteousness and peace for those who have been trained by it." – Hebrews 12:11 (NIV)

5. Extend Grace. None of us would be where we are today if God hadn't given us a second chance by sending His Son. Be quick to forgive, and always open to giving second chances. When team members mess up, use the moment to teach so long as they are willing to accept correction.

"Blessed are the merciful, for they will be shown mercy." – Matthew 5:7 (NIV)

6. Draw The Line. There comes a point where you've got to make some tough choices. You can only give a team member so many strikes before they have to be taken out of the game. If you can't cure the cancer, you need to cut it out before it becomes malignant and does even more damage.

"I urge you, brothers and sisters, to watch out for those who cause divisions and put obstacles in your way that are contrary to the teaching you have learned. Keep away from them." – Romans 16:17 (NIV)

7. Fess Up. Don't be afraid to admit you're wrong or apologize when you go overboard with your criticism. This requires that you overcome your pride, and that's never an easy thing to do. But it will create a strong bond with your team when you are able to be transparent and honest in your shortcomings as a leader.

"Whoever conceals their sins does not prosper, but the one who confesses and renounces them finds mercy." – Proverbs 28:13 (NIV)

STUDY QUESTIONS

1. What is your personal definition of the word "accountability?" Is this something that is actively going on in your life? Explain.

2. Can you describe a time when you needed to rely on some trusted voices in your life as either a leader or a team member? What was the result of that situation?

3. Why do you think accountability can sometimes be difficult for people in leadership? Why do you think accountability can sometimes be difficult for people who are under someone else's authority?

4. What are some common consequences for leaders or team members who don't exercise or submit to accountability?

5. When reading about Jesus' leadership, what aspects of how He modeled accountability stand out to you? Explain.

6. Of the seven keys to internal accountability, which ones have been beneficial to you as a leader or as a team member? Which ones have you struggled to apply to your life?

7. What are some things you can do today that will help you be more accountable to God, be more accountable to your earthly authority, and foster accountability amongst your team?

FOLLOW THROUGH

• Set your clock back five minutes to ensure that you are always on time.

• Identify an accountability partner, and meet with that person at least once a month.

• Join a small group or Bible study at your church or school.

• Print up or write out the Ten Commandments. Reflect on how each one can help you stay accountable to God and His biblical principles.

• Read through and meditate on the scriptures found throughout this chapter. If you'd like to do some additional Bible study on Community and accountability, here are some verses to get you started: Ecclesiastes 4:9, Romans 16:17, 2 Timothy 3:16-17.

PRAYER

Lord, guide my path to like-minded leaders who will hold me accountable to my promises and accountable for my actions. Humble my heart so that I might receive direction when needed and correction when required. Amen.

CHAPTER TEN: COMMUNITY III
BEING A SERVANT LEADER

"In the same way, let your light shine before others, that they may see your good deeds and glorify your Father in heaven."
–Matthew 5:16 (NIV)

Internal Community (or accountability) is vital to the long-term sustainability of any organization or team, but there's no point to building each other up and feeding each other's spiritual and emotional needs, if you aren't going to take that same attitude out into the real world.

To that end, it's your responsibility as the leader to model servant leadership. Sure, the people that you lead can do things in the Community on their own, but it's so much more powerful when they can see you at the front of the line, creating those opportunities for everyone to serve together.

Servant leadership is also connected to external Communication. If you want to get a positive message out to your audience, there's no better way than to show that community that you actually care about them as people and not just a target market. The act of serving is important, but what you leave behind is much more so.

SHOOT STRAIGHT

Throughout my career as a coach and teacher, I was always proactively involved in the community. Serving others was always important to me because of the importance my mother placed on serving others. No matter how much or little she had, she always felt it was a blessing for her to be able to lend someone else a helping hand. She thanked God for everything she had and loved cooking and delivering food to the elderly through the Meals On Wheels program. Because of her, I have always enjoyed giving as much, if not more, than I enjoyed being on the receiving end.

My dream job was to coach the varsity boys' basketball team at my alma mater, Rindge Technical High School, which was later renamed Cambridge Rindge and Latin. It took ten years to finally get that opportunity, but in the meantime I served as a physical education teacher while also working as an assistant coach at Northeastern University and Harvard.

During that time period, my good friend and fellow teacher, Joe Colannino, and I created the Shoot Straight Youth Basketball program, which was based on these seven key objectives:

1. To offer a positive team experience for boys and girls between the ages of seven and twelve years old.

2. To develop a systematic and educational approach to basketball, and show its correlation to learning.

3. To teach children the true meaning of teamwork, sportsmanship, cooperation, respect, and hard work.

4. To show the correlation between good team members and good citizens on and off the court.

5. To teach children the importance and necessity for rules and regulations, and how vitally important it is for them to respect the men and women that have to enforce them (referees and police officers).

6. To teach important life skills that they could use for a lifetime.

7. To create opportunities for youngsters to develop leadership skills.

One of the things that made Shoot Straight special was the fact that our players taught the fundamentals, coached the players, and refereed the games. The majority of our coaches started as seven and eight-year-old players. Many of them went on to play for me at the high school and become part of our coaching and leadership team.

The program was influential throughout the Community for a lot of reasons, but internally, it was just as beneficial to our players as it was to the aspiring athletes that it reached. The team (including future NBA Hall of Fame center, Patrick Ewing, and future NCAA champion, Rumeal Robinson) participated as players then coaches.

Forty years later, Shoot Straight continues under the direction of one of my former high school players, Lance Dottin, who started in the program at the age of seven. I would be remiss if I didn't mention he is also the head coach at Cambridge Rindge and Latin High School, and his teams have won two State Championships.

Not long ago, I watched a video featuring Anthony Colannino, the son of the program's co founder, Joe Colannino. As a little kid, Anthony was a participant in the program. In the video, he talked about how Shoot Straight helped him while his family was going through some tough times. He spoke about the calming influence that I had on him and how I helped him navigate through this difficult time in his life.

You usually don't know your positive effect on other people until much later. Sometimes you never know at all, and that's okay. The important thing to remember is that the simple act of serving will never be an empty proposition. As we meet the needs of kids in the community, we are able to deposit even more valuable messages and life lessons that last a lifetime.

SOLE PURPOSE

Throughout my journey, I've been blessed to encounter many great leaders who put the needs of the community first, and none exemplify the concept of servant leadership quite like Manny Ohonme.

Manny's approach to leadership is every bit as unique as his inspirational story, which is beautifully recounted in his best-selling book *Sole Purpose*. He didn't have much of anything as a young boy growing up in Lagos, Nigeria, but his mother made sure to help him envision a brighter future.

"The reason why God created the sky so high was so boys like you could dream real high," she told Manny.

Then, one hot summer afternoon, a missionary from Wisconsin showed up and invited him to enter a contest where the prize was a brand new pair of shoes. He could only imagine what that would be like, so he eagerly jumped at the chance to participate.

Manny won the contest, but it was the words of encouragement from the missionary that ultimately became a much greater reward than those shoes.

"Just because all you see around you is poverty doesn't mean the God of the universe has forgotten about you," the missionary said. "Keep dreaming, and dream big!"

Manny held onto the words of his mother and the missionary tightly.

"Sometimes I have to pinch myself to really think in terms of where I've come from," Manny said. "But I serve a God that had a plan for my life. In spite of the economic reality of my world, that didn't determine the altitude to which God has designed for me to live my life."

Manny put on those brand new shoes and ran—literally and metaphorically—toward his destiny. He worked hard in school, learned the game of basketball, and earned a full-ride scholarship to the University of North Dakota – Lake Region and later transferred to Concordia College in Moorhead, Minnesota, where he earned his degree. Manny also went on to earn his Masters at North Dakota State University and became a successful technology professional.

But that wasn't enough. Even after marrying and starting a family, Manny knew he had to do more. He never forgot about those shoes and the impact that one man made on his life. Manny didn't just want to be a leader. He wanted to be a *servant* leader.

After a trip back to Nigeria, Manny understood what he was called to do. In 2003, he and his wife, Tracie, started Samaritan's Feet, a 501(c)(3) humanitarian aid organization that, according to its website, "serves and inspires hope in children by providing shoes as the foundation to a spiritual and healthy life, resulting in the advancement of education and economic opportunities."

Since then, Manny's organization has served more than six and a half million people in ninety nations!

"I know what I've been given, which means I understand how important it is to give back," Manny said. "And not just because of a religious responsibility, but because it's a God ordained command. That's where I live my life. I want to pour myself out so I can become a reflection of what God can do. My life becomes a mirror to those kids so they can see hope through that lens. That's what we're trying to do."

Through the influence of Samaritan's Feet, Manny has been able to partner with numerous NBA and NCAA teams over the years. One of his most special relationships has been with University of Kentucky head coach, John Calipari. Coach Cal routinely invites Manny to speak to his players, so they can understand what it means to serve the community. Manny has even traveled with Kentucky and other teams on humanitarian trips around the world.

He is reminded often of something the iconic poet, Dr. Maya Angelou, once told him a few years before she passed away. "We need to be the rainbow in someone else's cloud," she said.

"Service to others emancipates humanity from the dungeon of self," Manny added. "I want people to know that this truth is the ultimate reason why I serve and should be the driving force that compels all of us to serve."

MIRACLES AND THE MESSAGE

If you're looking for an example of uncompromised servant leadership, there is none greater than Jesus Christ. Even though He was the most brilliant theological mind to inhabit the earth, Jesus wasn't holed up in the synagogue all day talking to the rabbis. Instead, He was always out in the Community, sharing stories from a mountainside, teaching biblical truths to a crowd on the seashore, meeting up with strangers at the local water well, attending weddings, or playing with children in the village.

But the crux of His ministry was all about meeting people's physical, emotional, and spiritual needs. In fact, it was Jesus' ability to do the miraculous that caught the public's attention and worked in tandem with His life-changing message about God's love. For instance, His second miracle (and first to take place publicly) occurred in Galilee where He healed a royal officer's son who was "close to death."

"Unless you people see signs and wonders," Jesus told him. "You will never believe." (John 4:48/NIV)

As more people saw and believed, the crowds that followed Him and listened to His teachings likewise grew. Not everyone who hung around, however, was interested in learning new things. Instead, many of the religious leaders were threatened and sought to discredit Jesus as a heretic or portray him as a fringe lunatic. Being in the Community and serving the people gave Him a chance to address those people as well.

In Matthew 12:9-14, we read about how Jesus healed a man with a shriveled hand on the Sabbath. This gave Him a chance to speak out against the Jewish teachers' legalistic interpretation of the law.

Looking for a reason to bring charges against Jesus, they asked him, "Is it lawful to heal on the Sabbath?" He said to them, "If any of you has a sheep and it falls into a pit on the Sabbath, will you not take hold of it and lift it out? How much more valuable is a person than a sheep! Therefore it is lawful to do good on the Sabbath." (Matthew 12:10-12/NIV)

Then in Mark 2:1-12, Jesus was teaching in a home, and it became so crowded that no one could get inside. Four men brought their paralytic friend on a mat and lowered him through a hole they made in the roof. They wanted Jesus to heal him, but first He forgave the man of his sins. This angered the other religious teachers in the room. Who had given this man the authority to do such a thing?

Immediately Jesus knew in his spirit that this was what they were thinking in their hearts, and he said to them, "Why are you thinking these things? Which is easier: to say to this paralyzed man, 'Your sins are forgiven,' or to say, 'Get up, take your mat and walk?' But I want you to know that the Son of Man has authority on earth to forgive sins." So he said to the man, "I tell you, get up, take your mat, and go home." He got up, took his mat and walked out in full view of them all. This amazed everyone, and they praised God, saying, "We have never seen anything like this!" (Mark 2:8-12/NIV)

Even though Jesus had an eternally important job, He was never oblivious to what the people were going through on a personal level. On two separate occasions (Matthew 15:32-39 and John 6:1-15), the Bible tells us how He took a small amount of food (some fish and a few loaves of bread) and multiplied it so that thousands of hungry people who had been listening to Him teach could be fed. It was a simple thing that gave Jesus yet another chance to validate His standing as the Son of God.

As He often did, Jesus explained the purpose behind servant leadership in smaller group discussions with His disciples. It must have been astonishing to hear the Son of God made flesh talking about the importance of putting others first. Of all people, Jesus should have been served, but here He was, telling His followers the exact opposite.

But Jesus called them together and said, "You know that the rulers in this world lord it over their people, and officials flaunt their authority over those under them. But among you it will be different. Whoever wants to be a leader among you must be your servant, and whoever wants to be first among you must become your slave. For even the Son of Man came not to be served but to serve others and to give his life as a ransom for many." (Matthew 20:25-28/NLT)

If anyone could have rightfully demanded to be served, it was Jesus Christ who wasn't just any man. He was the Son of God. Yet here He was preaching a very different message than we often hear from people in high places of authority and power. There's no way to be a truly great leader if you aren't a *servant* leader.

TAKING IT TO THE STREETS

Jesus set an example that His disciples followed in the immediate days after His ascension into Heaven and continued to exemplify for the next several years. This was especially the case as it pertained to impacting the external community. As the disciples transitioned into their roles as apostles and leaders of the Early Church, they continued Jesus' legacy of performing miracles and serving people's needs. And just like Jesus, their servant leadership opened the door to communicating a much greater message.

In Acts 2, the Holy Spirit descended upon the disciples as they gathered, just as Jesus had promised. This was their sign to begin taking the gospel message to the streets. The Early Church quickly grew to over three thousand believers.

But again, just like Jesus, they did so as active participants in the public square. They went out into the community and met people's needs, such as the crippled beggar who had been unable to walk from birth. He asked Peter and John for money, but they had nothing monetary to give him. Instead, they relied on the Holy Spirit to give him something even better.

Then Peter said, "Silver or gold I do not have, but what I do have I give you. In the name of Jesus Christ of Nazareth, walk." Taking him by the right hand, he helped him up, and instantly the man's feet and ankles became strong. He jumped to his feet and began to walk. Then he went with them into the temple courts, walking and jumping, and praising God. When all the people saw him walking and praising God, they recognized him as the same man who used to sit begging at the temple gate called Beautiful, and they were filled with wonder and amazement at what had happened to him. (Acts 3:6-10/NIV)

This gave Peter the chance to speak to the crowds that began to gather and opened the door to sharing his message with the local leaders. Because of that miracle, another two thousand people joined the ranks of the Early Church (Acts 4:4).

Sometimes being in the community can bring adversity your way. There may be some who oppose your message. There may be others who see you as a threat to their territory. So don't be surprised when activating servant leadership isn't always a welcome sight. This was certainly the case with Jesus and the apostles. Jesus' works put His message in the spotlight, and those who disagreed with what He was saying worked to remove Him from the scene. Peter's exploits cost him his life. John was exiled to a deserted island. The apostle Paul survived many assassination attempts before eventually dying at the opposition's hands.

So don't be surprised if not everyone basks in the glow of your good deeds. It won't likely bear the same consequences as the Early Christians, but rest assured that as long as your message is based in truth, meeting needs in the community will always produce fruit, whether you see it right away or not.

SEVEN KEYS TO EXTERNAL COMMUNICATION (OR BEING A SERVANT LEADER)

Being an effective leader requires time behind a desk, time alone, time with the team, etc., but you can't stay there too long, or you will become stagnant. It's important to get out in public and serve those around you. The end result isn't just about making you feel good about yourself or even making an individual's life better for that moment in time. It's about trying to help people see the truth and help them see their own potential and purpose.

Just like Jesus gave sight to the blind, we are called to help people see what they can do and what they are called to do. That's doing God's work. And so often it comes in the form of reaching out and getting involved in the Community. With that in mind, here are seven keys that will help you become a better servant leader:

1. Discover Your Gifts. When God created you He gave you special gifts that were intended for the benefit of others. Part of serving means recognizing and understanding (and then honing) the talents and abilities that are encoded into your DNA. If you've never taken an aptitude test, we've placed one in the appendix at the back of the book that will help you discover your gifts and empower you to use them.

"God has given each of you a gift from his great variety of spiritual gifts. Use them well to serve one another." (1 Peter 4:10/NLT)

2. Be Moved By Compassion. Motivation is everything when it comes to servant leadership. Make sure you're doing it for the right reasons. There should be no personal agenda—just loving people and building God's Kingdom. This requires Christ-like humility and godly compassion.

"For even the Son of Man came not to be served but to serve others and to give his life as a ransom for many." (Matthew 20:28/NLT)

3. Know Your Surroundings. Do some reconnaissance work. Get out there and talk to people. See what's going on in your Community. Assess the situation. Then, you'll be better equipped to meet whatever needs there might be.

"I tell you, open your eyes and look at the fields! They are ripe for harvest." (John 4:35b/NIV)

4. Make A Plan. With guidance from the Holy Spirit, write down the things you hope to accomplish, and then start mapping out the logistics of how that plan can be implemented. If the plan isn't successful, start over until you get it right.

"But don't begin until you count the cost. For who would begin construction of a building without first calculating the cost to see if there is enough money to finish it? Otherwise, you might complete only the foundation before running out of money, and then everyone would laugh at you. They would say, 'There's the person who started that building and couldn't afford to finish it!'" (Luke 14:28-30/NLT)

5. Build Your Team. You can't do it alone. Find likeminded people within your organization or group to help you implement the plan—people that will buy into the mission and help you accomplish the goal. Anything I've done that's turned out well has been in conjunction with other people helping me. The same is true for all leaders.

"Just as a body, though one, has many parts, but all its many parts form one body, so it is with Christ...Even so the body is not made up of one part but of many." (1 Corinthians 12:12, 14/NIV)

6. Be Consistent. Make serving others a part of your routine, and when you start something, don't quit when things get difficult. Consistency curries long-term favor in the community. Bailing on your Commitment will not only discourage those in need, but it can also leave a vacuum for people to fill that void with the wrong message.

"And as for you, brothers and sisters, never tire of doing what is good." (2 Thessalonians 3:13/NIV)

7. Make It Sustainable. The ultimate goal is to build something that will last and can be shared for generations to come, and perhaps expanded beyond your Community for the greatest impact possible. Just as Jesus empowered His disciples to continue His work, we as leaders must also help others replicate the work and keep it going when you are gone. This is the legacy of servant leadership.

"In the same way, let your light shine before others, that they may see your good deeds and glorify your Father in heaven." (Matthew 5:16/NIV)

STUDY QUESTIONS

1. How do you define the term "servant leadership?"

2. What are some of the factors that might make it difficult for people to act as servant leaders in today's society?

3. What inspiration do you draw from the example of Jesus and the apostles?

4. What are some specific ways that external Communication (taking a message to your audience) and external Community (being a servant leader) are connected?

5. Why do you think it's important to know your gifts, talents, and abilities? How do you think knowing those things about yourself can help you become a better servant leader?

6. Of the seven keys listed, which have you been able to implement as a leader? Which have been difficult to implement? How has the implementation (or lack thereof) of those keys positively or negatively impacted your ability to serve?

7. What are some things you can start doing today that will help you to become a more effective servant leader?

FOLLOW THROUGH

• Eliminate something in your daily life (i.e. coffee, ice cream, junk food, entertainment, etc.) and donate that money to your favorite charity.

• Go through your closet and donate your unused clothing to an organization that clothes the poor.

• Donate your time, talent, and treasure to an organization that helps the less fortunate or makes a positive impact on the Community. Here are a few that you may want to partner with:

  • Samaritan's Feet
  • Salvation Army
  • Food For The Hungry
  • Meals On Wheels
  • The Dream Center
  • The Walk USA
  • Upward Youth Sports
  • Boys & Girls Club of America

• Exercise your right to vote in every election.

• Engage in civil discussions with your family, friends, neighbors, and co-workers about community issues, politics, and faith.

• Read through and meditate on the scriptures found throughout this chapter. If you'd like to do some additional Bible study on serving the Community, here are some verses to get you started: Matthew 5:16, Matthew 20:28, 1 Peter 4:10.

PRAYER

Lord, give me a heart for my Community. Reveal to me the problems, and empower me to be part of the solution. Give me a vision for the most effective ways to serve others, and bring to me the people who will make up a strong, committed team. I want to bless others as a living testimony of Your amazing love. Amen.

CHAPTER ELEVEN: COACH I
BEING MENTORED

"Walk with the wise and become wise; associate with fools and get in trouble."
–Proverbs 13:20 (NLT)

It doesn't matter if you aspire to be an influential leader or if you're already operating at a high level of authority, you're always going to need someone to Coach you up or mentor you along the way. It makes no difference how much you think you know, you'll never know it all—and you'll certainly never stop learning how to be a better leader.

COURSE DIRECTION

God has always put people in my life whose primary role was to mentor me. There were many times when I resisted or even rejected being mentored. Thankfully, on three occasions in particular, I was smart enough to recognize the value of some very wise counsel and direction.

One of my first mentors was someone who was very close to me—my older brother, Richard. I don't think I truly realized how much he loved me until he was gone. Looking back, I can see so many times that he sacrificed his own dreams and ambitions for the rest of the family.

Richard didn't have the opportunities that I was afforded. He didn't get to lead the life of a young boy wanting to play sports. Instead, he was responsible for helping my mother feed and clothe the rest of us. Richard willingly gave up his athletic career even though he had far and above the most potential. I jokingly called him the "white sheep of the family." He was 6 foot3 inches and didn't have an ounce of body fat.

Because Richard wasn't able to play sports, he understood how valuable that experience was for me. He saw things in me that I didn't usually see in myself, like my stubbornness. He would tell me what God wanted me to hear—and I wasn't always receptive to the message. I thought Richard was overcritical, but looking back, I can see that he was just painfully honest with me. He wanted me to be the best that I could be and experience some of the things he dreamt about.

Richard could be tough on me sometimes. He paid attention to the details like whether or not I washed my hands before dinner or how fast I ate and how much I ate. I ate fast and I ate a lot. Therefore, I was overweight as a youngster. Richard wanted to help me correct those negative traits so I could be my very best.

Then, when I quit the Northeastern University basketball team, he gave me a job at his fish and chips store, so he could mentor me some more and talk me into going back to school. He was the one who guided my return back to Northeastern, which laid the foundation for my future as a teacher and a coach. Richard even drove sometimes up to 250 miles one way to watch me mostly sit on the bench.

Richard's mentoring didn't end when I graduated from college. Deep into my coaching career, he was still watching from close by and giving me much needed counsel. Richard realized that he hadn't always led me in a loving way, so when he saw me being too harsh with my players, he suggested that maybe I should change my approach.

I considered Richard to be a mentor until the day he passed away in 2002. Like I said before, it wasn't until then that I fully understood and appreciated just how much his guidance and direction changed the course of my life.

Another influential mentor that helped shape my future was Dick Dukeshire, my head coach at Northeastern University. After my brother, Richard, steered me back to the basketball program there, I became intentional about being mentored to be a great coach and teacher. I still didn't get much playing time, but I developed a different relationship with Coach Dukeshire and took the opportunity to study his coaching style.

As I mentioned in chapter one, it was during those formative years that I decided to become a head coach with the goal of returning to my high school alma mater—Rindge Technical High School—to teach Physical Education and build one of the best high school basketball programs in the country. I wanted to do for those kids what wasn't done for me. I wanted to teach them not only how to play basketball the correct way, but also to make sure they had the grades to make it to college. I think Coach Dukeshire took heart in the fact that I wanted to be mentored by him. He started to look at me in a different light.

When I didn't get the high school job immediately, I went back to Northeastern and served as an assistant coach while teaching at the high school. I had daily opportunities to be mentored and to learn how to run a successful program from one of New England's all-time greats.

Many of Coach Dukeshire's players became coaches. I was one of those former players blessed to be prominently mentioned in his obituary. Prior to his passing, Coach Dukeshire shared his pride in how far I had gone in my career. Even better, his mentoring influenced a complainer and troublemaker in the locker room to become the most treasured branch of his coaching tree.

Being mentored isn't just for the purpose of developing life skills or for the purpose of career advancement. In fact, I would argue that the greatest need in a mentoring relationship is to have someone who will give you spiritual guidance and teach you what it means to follow Christ.

For me, one of the most important mentors in my life was a man named David Nicholas. He was my pastor at Spanish River Community Church in Boca Raton, Florida, and the person responsible for leading me to the Lord.

I'll talk more about Pastor Nicholas in chapter thirteen, but I wanted to mention him to make the point that you should likewise find someone who is more concerned with the condition of your soul than the size of your platform or the contents of your wallet. I'm thankful that I had these three men (and many others) that taught me the truth about life (like my brother, Richard), the truth about my career (like Coach Dukeshire), and most importantly, the truth about my eternal future (like Pastor Nicholas).

TAKING THE MANTLE

Throughout the entire Bible, there are many great examples of mentoring. One of the most compelling such stories can be found in parts of 1 and 2 Kings where a powerful prophet named Elijah trained a young man named Elisha to take his place.

Long before Elisha entered the picture, Elijah had gained a reputation as one of God's chosen spokesmen—His voice to the people and His word of warning to the kings. Elijah became famous for performing breathtaking miracles including the calling down of fire in 1 Kings 18.

Shortly after, however, God spoke to Elijah and instructed him to seek out Elisha who at the time was working his wealthy father's land. When Elijah arrived at Elisha's home, he was plowing the field like any other day. Elijah went up to Elisha and threw his cloak around his shoulders. Elisha must have recognized Elijah, because he immediately left his oxen and ran after the prophet.

"Let me kiss my father and mother goodbye," he said. "And then I will come with you." (1 Kings 19:20b/NIV)

Elisha took his commitment to Elijah one step further. He slaughtered his cattle, burned the plow, cooked the meat, and served it to the other workers. For the next seven or eight years, Elisha followed Elijah and learned from him, but the Bible says nothing about the young protégé during that time. It's almost as if he was invisible or in the shadows. Yet, we know Elisha is waiting in the wings and being faithful to the process.

In 2 Kings, Elijah uses his rolled up mantle to divide the waters of the Jordan River so he and Elisha can cross to the other side. "Tell me, what can I do for you before I am taken from you?" Elijah asks Elisha.

"Let me inherit a double portion of your spirit," Elisha replied.

A few moments later, Elijah is miraculously ushered up to heaven in a whirlwind. His mantle falls to the ground and Elisha claims it as his own and uses it to part the waters and cross back to the other side of the Jordan River. (2 Kings 2:7-14/NIV)

It was now Elisha's time, and because of his faithfulness, he did even more miracles than Elijah. He served as a prophet in Israel for sixty years and served as an advisor for four kings. Elijah purified Jericho's unclean waters (2 Kings 2:21), cured a leper's diseased body (2 Kings 5), put an end to the nation's grievous idol worship (2 Kings 10:28), and raised a boy from the dead (2 Kings 4:18-37).

The only reason Elisha did all of these things is because he was willing to follow after Elijah, and he was willing to stay in the shadows while learning from his mentor. When Elijah's mantle fell to the ground, Elisha was ready to take it and become the leader that God had called him to be.

TEACHING THE TEACHER

It sounds a little strange to say this, but did you know that even Jesus took time to be mentored? Even though He was fully God, He was also fully human, and had to experience life. Jesus patiently waited thirty years before He started His ministry. Even during His youth, the Bible tells us that He took time to study the Hebrew Scriptures.

In one story, a twelve-year-old Jesus got separated from his parents during the Festival of the Passover. On their way home, they realized He was no longer with the group that was traveling together. A frantic search revealed that Jesus was "in the temple courts, sitting among the teachers, listening to them, and asking them questions." (Luke 2:46/NIV)

Jesus continued to be mentored during His ministry. While there was no one on earth capable of giving Him perfect wisdom and instruction, He did have a direct line of communication with God the Father. Talking to God was something Jesus did on a daily basis. For instance, "Very early in the morning, while it was still dark, Jesus got up, left the house, and went off to a solitary place, where he prayed." (Mark 1:35/NIV)

Then, in the final week before His crucifixion, Jesus stole away to the Garden of Gethsemane with His disciples to spend time talking to God. The disciples fell asleep as Jesus received final confirmation that His mission had not changed.

"My Father, if it is possible, may this cup be taken from me. Yet not as I will, but as you will." (Matthew 26:39/NIV)

If Jesus, the Great Teacher, submitted to mentoring from His Father, how much more important it must be for us to find godly men and women who can teach us, train us, and impart into us the wisdom we need to become strong, effective leaders.

SEVEN KEYS TO BEING MENTORED

There's no question that I would not be here today if it weren't for the mentors who took the time to guide my steps and teach me about life. The same is true for anyone who wants to be a leader. It is simply impossible to get there without help from capable, knowledgeable, and wise voices speaking into your spirit.

If you're ready to take the next step in your leadership journey, here are seven keys to finding a coach and allowing him or her to mentor you:

1. Recognize The Need. Honesty is the first step to being mentored. It required self-evaluation and the understanding that you have strengths that can be made stronger and weaknesses that need to be shored up.

"Examine me, LORD, and inspect me! Test my heart and mind." *(Psalm 26:2/ISV)*

2. Be Humble. You're not perfect. No one is, not even those whom you might call upon to be your mentor. Admit that you don't have all the answers, and prepare your heart to receive the training and guidance that will help make you a better leader.

"So humble yourselves under the mighty power of God, and at the right time he will lift you up in honor." (1 Peter 5:6/NLT)

3. Look Around. Be intentional in seeking a mentor. It might be someone close to you or someone you can observe from afar. It might be someone God has already placed in your life or a new acquaintance that has just the advice and direction that you need.

"Walk with the wise and become wise; associate with fools and get in trouble." (Proverbs 13:20/NLT)

4. Soak It Up. When you spend time with your mentor, pay close attention to what they say. Take good notes, and ask lots of questions. Communicate regularly, openly, and honestly. You might not always have that person with you, but you can still lean on their wisdom even when they aren't around.

"My son, pay attention to what I say; turn your ear to my words. Do not let them out of your sight, keep them within your heart; for they are life to those who find them and health to one's whole body." (Proverbs 4:20-22/NIV)

5. Be Faithful. Stick with your Commitment. Being mentored isn't always an easy process. A good mentor will tell you things you don't want to hear. You have to be prepared to take the bad with the good. Don't allow the difficult aspects of being mentored cause you to become discouraged or to give up. You've got to stick with it.

"Therefore, my dear friends, as you have always obeyed—not only in my presence, but now much more in my absence—continue to work out your salvation with fear and trembling, for it is God who works in you to will and to act in order to fulfill his good purpose." *(Philippians 2:12-13/NIV)*

6. Wait Your Turn. If you have yet to reach the level of leadership that you desire, be patient for your opportunity, and appreciate the mentoring process that is helping you get there. It took me ten years to get the coaching job at Cambridge. I could have taken a different route in order to speed things up, but God knew I was going to need all of that time to prepare. It's okay to wait. The right mentors in your life will make sure you're ready when it's your turn.

"But if we hope for what we do not yet have, we wait for it patiently." *(Romans 8:25/NIV)*

7. Repeat The Process. You may have a mentor for a season in your life. Don't trick yourself into thinking that you've done enough once a mentoring relationship has ended. Find new mentors to fill the gaps. Study and read what other great leaders have to say. It's a continuous process that will always move you forward.

"A wise man will hear and increase in learning, and a man of understanding will acquire wise counsel." *(Proverbs 1:5/NASB)*

STUDY QUESTIONS

1. Who are some people that you would say have been influential mentors in your life? What are the most important things you learned from them?

2. Do you currently have an active mentor in your life? If so, how has it helped you become a better leader? If not, what has kept you from doing so?

3. Do you think you should wait for a mentor to approach you, or do you think it's more appropriate to ask someone to be your mentor? Explain.

4. What are your thoughts after reading about Jesus and His approach to being mentored?

5. What do you think are some attributes that a good mentor should have? How might having that kind of mentor make a positive impact on your life?

6. What are some challenges that you've personally faced when trying to have someone mentor you? Have you been able to overcome those challenges? Explain.

7. What is something you can do today that will help you better utilize the concept of mentoring in your life?

FOLLOW THROUGH

• Find a mentor and commit to meeting with him or her at least once a month.

• Read through and meditate on the scriptures found throughout this chapter. If you'd like to do some additional Bible study on being mentored, here are some verses to get you started: Proverbs 1:5, Proverbs 4:20-22, Proverbs 13:20.

PRAYER

Lord, I know that I cannot make it on my own. Help me recognize my shortcomings, and bring people into my life who can mentor me and make me a stronger leader. Give me a humble heart that is pliable and teachable. Give me the patience to endure the process and to understand that where You are taking me is far greater than where I am today. Amen.

CHAPTER TWELVE: COACH II
BEING A MENTOR

"Instruct the wise, and they will be even wiser. Teach the righteous, and they will learn even more."
–Proverbs 9:9 (NLT)

One of the most rewarding aspects of leadership is being a mentor. It's an incredible feeling when you realize that you have positively impacted someone's life forever. But that's not why all leaders should also be mentors. No, leaders should be mentors because that's what we are made to do. Leadership is a gift from God, but it is intended to come from a position of serving—just like Jesus came to serve us.

Leaders, however, should appreciate mentoring for another reason—because we all have people in our lives that influenced, inspired, and served us. Some nights I have trouble sleeping because I can't stop thinking about all of the incredible men and women that have mentored me—my mother, my brothers, my sister, my wife, my teachers, my coaches, and my peers. They had so much influence on my life. They prepared me, nurtured me, and gave me the foundation I needed to be successful.

Such is our responsibility as leaders. We should be working to bring the best out in others, helping them discover their special gifts, and teaching them how to hone their unique talents. God is calling all of us to pass our experience, knowledge, and wisdom from this generation to the next with the hope of ushering in a better world.

FROM INVENTOR TO MENTOR

If you've studied the history of basketball, you probably already know that James Naismith invented the game during his time at Springfield College in Springfield, Massachusetts—1891 to be exact. Even the casual fan has likely heard his last name mentioned in reference to the Naismith College Player of the Year award and the Naismith Memorial Basketball Hall of Fame.

But what many don't know is that the Scottish-Canadian physical education teacher created the game as a way to keep his students occupied during the cold, winter months and ultimately viewed athletics as a way to instill biblical values in young men.

That's why as you dive into the Naismith story, it surprisingly has little to do with his famous invention. At his core, everything he did was more about building relationships and perpetuating opportunities to mentor those within his circle of influence.

Perhaps the best example can be found later in Naismith's life. It was in 1932 when he was serving as an administrator at Kansas University. A young, African American man named John McClendon walked into his office one day with an unusual request. His father had instructed him to go to Naismith if he needed any help.

It was the kind of opportunity that the wise professor wholeheartedly embraced—even though segregation was still the cultural and legal norm of the day. Naismith took McClendon under his wing and welcomed him into the physical education program. Over the next four years, not only did he spend one-on-one time with the young man, but he also defended him when faced with injustice and humiliating circumstances.

Naismith's efforts paid off in a big way. McClendon went on to become a pioneering basketball coach who today is credited as the creator of the four corners offense, the fast break, and the full court press. As one of the most prominent African American coaches of his day, McClendon became an inspiration to countless up-and-coming coaches such as myself. And much of his rise to prominence can be attributed back to Naismith's willingness to mentor and build up the next generation of leaders.

PASSING THE BALL

In 1974, I was teaching physical education at my alma mater, Rindge Technical High School, in Cambridge, Massachusetts. I was also working as an assistant men's basketball coach at Harvard University under former Celtics great, Tom "Satch" Sanders.

It was a sunny, fall day, and I just finished teaching one of my morning P.E. classes when my good friend and fellow P.E. teacher, Steve Jenkins, introduced me to a seventh grader named Patrick Ewing who had just moved from Jamaica to Cambridge. Patrick was about 6 foot3 inches, very thin, very shy, and had a heavy Jamaican accent.

Steve coached football, and like Patrick, who grew up playing cricket and soccer, knew very little about basketball. Steve asked me if I would do him a favor and tutor him and Patrick about the game and how it should be played. Soon thereafter, I started working with Patrick and Steve on the fundamentals of basketball, such as dribbling, passing and shooting, and how a big man was supposed to play.

While I was working privately with Patrick during the day and coaching at Harvard at night, I had no idea that four years later I would be his high school coach. Our first year together as player and coach was Patrick's sophomore year. He was 6 foot 9 inches and weighed 165 pounds. By the time he was a senior, he was seven feet tall, weighed 235 pounds, and had developed into the most dominant high school basketball player in America.

Together, we recorded an almost perfect record of 77-1 and became the #1-ranked team in the nation. Every game we played, including our contests at the Boston Garden, were sold out. When Patrick went to Georgetown University, he was ready to compete and win at the highest level. He was a three-time all-American, played in three national championship games, was the 1984 National Player of the Year, and the key player on the Hoyas' 1984 NCAA Championship team.

A few months after Patrick graduated from Georgetown in 1985, he became the first NBA Lottery draft selection when the New York Knicks selected him with the #1 pick. Patrick spent seventeen years in the NBA (mostly with the New York Knicks) where he was 1986 Rookie of the Year, an 11-time All-Star, and two-time Olympic gold medalist.

In 2008, I was in attendance when Patrick received the ultimate honor of being inducted into the Naismith Basketball Hall of Fame in Springfield, Massachusetts. Since retiring as a player, Patrick spent time as a successful NBA assistant coach and was most recently named head men's basketball coach at Georgetown.

As one of his first mentors, I'm proud of what he accomplished as a player and coach, but I'm more proud of the kind of person he has become. Patrick is a man of character who values loyalty, honesty, and hard work. He loves his family and understands what it means to be a leader.

Patrick was just one of the many young people I was blessed to mentor. My goal was to provide all of them the father figure that I didn't always have. I wanted them to see a strong, loving, caring person that wasn't afraid to tell them what they needed to hear as opposed to what they wanted to hear. I wanted them to understand and appreciate the value of work. I wanted them to understand the importance of being a good teammate and how a group of people can achieve great things if they have a common goal and a common purpose.

Then, I wanted them to pass that knowledge and wisdom on to their children and on to others in the Community.

Nearly forty years after I first met Patrick, I found myself in a locker room at the University of Texas at El Paso where my Florida Atlantic squad had just been eliminated from the Conference USA tournament. I knew that I would not be returning to coach at FAU, and that this was the last time they would hear me give a postgame talk. I wanted it to be something they would remember. As I stood at the front of the room, I shared this message:

"Gentlemen, when you leave this program, I hope and pray that you will find an incredible woman to marry and that you will be blessed with loving children. Furthermore, I hope you will be a great husband—and all-American dad."

I then asked the team to huddle up, and I closed the talk with a prayer.

As I spoke these words, my son, Mike Jr., was standing nearby, just like he always had during the majority of my coaching career. In fact, by the time Mike Jr. was three, he was serving as the batboy on my freshman high school baseball team. Seven years later at the age of ten, he assumed the position of ball boy at Cambridge and was at my side for all three of our championship photos.

After his college basketball career (where he played for me at Boston University), Mike Jr. joined my staff at George Washington University, and we became the first African American father-son coaching duo in NCAA history. He stayed with me until that final stop at FAU.

Mike Jr. always had my back, and I had his. I always respected the fact that Mike wasn't afraid to tell me the truth, whether I liked it or not. We made a great team. When we were together, I always felt like anything was possible.

But more than anything, I relished my role as Mike's mentor. I wanted to be the dad to him that I wish my dad had been to me. If I died today, I would feel very good about having accomplished what I was supposed to accomplish. I taught him how to be a father and what love is all about.

I've seen Mike grow into an incredible man, husband, and father. He's a very successful businessman, and he has great relationships that have lasted for decades. I've seen him deal with both success and adversity, but most importantly, I've seen him make the commitment that took me sixty years to make—the Commitment to follow Christ. That was the greatest reward and trophy that any dad could receive.

SKILLS FOR LIFE

In 1985, I became even more intentional about mentoring others. While the opportunity to lead the young men around me was a blessing of the highest order, I still felt like there was more that I could do with the platform I had been given.

That motivated me to develop a book and curriculum called *Skills For Life*. The purpose was to convey practical wisdom to young people who wanted to succeed. I enlisted the help of my good friend, Jonathan Peck, a successful business consultant who worked with me to develop a unique program to teach the fundamentals needed to face the real world with confidence and enthusiasm.

In many ways, the concept behind *Skills For Life* wasn't too different from the basic idea behind this book. It revolved around the following topics:

- Character
- Attitude
- Getting Along
- [a] Spirituality
- Appearance/Costume
- Basic Communication
- Work With A Plan
- Matters of Money
- Giving Back
- The Best You Can Be

As Jonathan and I promoted the book, one of our primary goals was to help bridge the gap between the serious disconnect that was impeding the passage of conventional wisdom from generation to generation. We had observed that a breakdown in communication had resulted in the failure of many people to learn the behaviors and thought processes that lead to success and satisfaction in school, at work, and in the home.

It's still a problem today. Households struggle to maintain financial equilibrium. Test result driven classrooms and business enterprises focus on the bottom line and create environments in which little time exists for teachers to teach and for students to learn the fundamentals of life. Without learning those life skills and fostering good habits, young people find it harder to succeed academically, financially, relationally, and spiritually.

That was the inspiration for *Skills For Life* and my second book, *Everybody Needs A Head Coach*. It continues to also be the inspiration for this book as well. And while not everyone will write a book, everyone can lead in this area and help teach young people, or even their peers, through personal mentoring. This is a vital activity for the future of our society, and something I hope every reader will consider doing for someone else.

PASSING THE STAFF

Moses is arguably one of the greatest leaders to walk the face of the earth. He brought an entire nation out of slavery, communicated directly with God, and guided the Israelites to safety.

But Moses wasn't perfect. He made some significant mistakes along the way, including one that cost him dearly. In Numbers 20:2-12, God instructed Moses to speak to a rock so it would pour out water for the complaining Israelites. But in his frustration, Moses struck the rock with his staff instead. Water gushed from the rock, but because Moses disobeyed God's specific command and showed a lack of faith, he was not allowed to enter the Promised Land.

Prior to Moses' disobedience, he had been mentoring a young man named Joshua. It's not likely that Moses was purposefully training Joshua and preparing him for a future leadership role. But rather, the relationship was born out of necessity. Moses needed help, and he allowed Joshua to be a part of his daily routine. This led to some amazing opportunities for Joshua, including the chance to lead a group of spies into Canaan (Numbers 13:16) and a life-changing encounter with God (Exodus 24:13-14).

Moses and Joshua's relationship was mutually beneficial. It was Moses' responsibility to pass the staff of leadership and prepare the next generation for the future. Joshua, on the other hand, was able to watch a seasoned leader in action. He gained valuable wisdom and knowledge from someone who had been tried and tested.

Moses knew he wasn't going to the Promised Land, but he humbled himself and willingly trained the young man who would take the staff and reap the benefit of Moses' labor.

As we later read in the Book of Joshua, Moses did his job well. The Israelites were in capable hands as their new leader guided them through many victorious battles and directed their path into Canaan. Moses set an example that all other mentors can continue to follow.

PASSING THE TORCH

Effective leaders don't just communicate their message. They observe. They listen. They craft responses that will bring greater understanding. That's how Jesus—the greatest mentor history has known—interacted with His disciples, because He saw the big picture and knew they would soon be carrying His message around the world.

Here are a few things we can learn from Jesus the mentor:

1. **He humbled Himself.** Even though Jesus was fully God *and* fully man, He didn't lead in a domineering fashion. He knew that God's plan was to use ordinary, everyday people to share the message of love, hope, and redemption. (Philippians 2:5-8)

2. **He sought them out.** Jesus didn't wait for people to come to Him requesting a mentoring relationship. He recruited them and looked for people who were willing to drop everything they were doing in order to follow Him and learn from Him. (Luke 5:1-11)

3. **He disciplined them.** When necessary, Jesus rebuked the disciples for saying and doing things that were contrary to His message. He was sometimes stern but always loving. Jesus understood that firm discipline was always in their best interest. (Luke 9:54-55)

4. **He listened and observed.** Jesus paid attention to what was going on around Him. Even when the disciples thought they were arguing in private, He was always attentive to their

conversations. This allowed Him to discipline when necessary, but mostly to take the opportunity to share His divine wisdom. (Luke 9:46-48)

5. **He went deeper.** Jesus mostly shared parables with the masses in order to give them a palatable version of the message. Then, He would pull the disciples aside and explain to them the deeper meaning behind those stories. (Mark 4:33-34)

6. **He entrusted them**. Ultimately, Jesus knew that the disciples would become the founding fathers of the Christian church. Just before He ascended into Heaven after His death and resurrection, He gave them instructions on what to do in the coming days. Jesus' time as their mentor was over, and it was their turn to take the message to the ends of the earth. (Matthew 28:19-20)

7. **He loved them**. He asked them to love their neighbors as they loved themselves. (Matthew 22:38-39)

If Jesus understood and exercised the role of mentoring during His ministry, it's difficult to deny that we too should do the same no matter what stage of leadership we might currently be walking out. Because Jesus chose to be a mentor, the world received His life-saving message.

Today, we have a choice to either follow Jesus' example or to fall back into selfishness and pride. I hope that you will join me in taking up the divinely created role of mentoring. Together we can make a difference in our communities and in our world.

SEVEN KEYS TO BEING A COACH (OR BEING A MENTOR)

Mentoring has great rewards. While that shouldn't be our motivation, I can speak from personal experience that bringing up the next generation of leaders can satisfy the soul. It doesn't get any better than that.

More importantly, mentoring is a God-given responsibility. There's so much chaos in our world, so much hopelessness in our communities, and too many of our children are born into dysfunctional homes. The lack of leadership and fathers in the home has caused a lot of problems, because that's where the real teaching and mentoring is supposed to begin and end.

It doesn't matter if you are a parent or the leader of an organization, mentoring others must be an intentional part of your daily life. Here are some ways to embrace that role and become more effective in doing so:

1. Exercise Humility. See the big picture. Your influence as a leader isn't meant to enrich your life, but to enrich the lives of others. Don't be threatened by those who you are leading. See them as the key aspects of a brighter future and not as someone who is angling to take your position.

"Do nothing out of selfish ambition or vain conceit. Rather, in humility value others above yourselves, not looking to your own interests but each of you to the interests of the others. In your relationships with one another, have the same mindset as Christ Jesus." *(Philippians 2:3-5/NIV)*

2. Understand The Value. Have a vision and a plan for being a mentor. Realize that it's a part of your role as a leader. Take it seriously. Recognize that you are responsible to help others fulfilling their callings.

"Instruct the wise, and they will be even wiser. Teach the righteous, and they will learn even more." – Proverbs 9:9 (NLT)

3. Recognize Opportunities. Mentoring is a two-way street. Be intentional about looking for someone to mentor, but also make yourself open, available, and ready for someone to approach you. Also, think outside the box and get involved with small groups or find ways to mentor larger audiences through podcasts, social media, and speaking engagements.

"Be shepherds of God's flock that is under your care, watching over them—not because you must, but because you are willing, as God wants you to be; not pursuing dishonest gain, but eager to serve; not lording it over those entrusted to you, but being examples to the flock." *(1 Peter 5:2-3/NIV)*

4. Be Committed. Invest your time, resources, and emotional energy to those you are mentoring. It's not easy, but sticking with it and persevering through adversity is a non-negotiable once you step into that role. Whatever you give as a mentor, God will abundantly give back to you.

"Give, and you will receive. Your gift will return to you in full—pressed down, shaken together to make room for more, running over, and poured into your lap. The amount you give will determine the amount you get back." (Luke 6:38/NLT)

5. Show That You Care. Be compassionate in your leadership but also willing to discipline them and keep them accountable to the process.

"Whoever loves discipline loves knowledge, but whoever hates correction is stupid." (Proverbs 12:1/NIV)

6. Be A Good Listener. Ask good questions and then take time to evaluate responses. Give your undivided attention. This helps you get to know someone better and allows for deeper, more meaningful dialogue.

"Spouting off before listening to the facts is both shameful and foolish." (Proverbs 18:13/NLT)

7. Repeat The Process. Never stop mentoring. Keep looking for more opportunities to speak into the lives of those around you. God didn't put us on earth to retire, sit on the beach, and play golf. He put us here to plant seeds. Serving others as a mentor is the only way to truly leave a legacy that will outlive you.

"So, my dear brothers and sisters, be strong and immovable. Always work enthusiastically for the Lord, for you know that nothing you do for the Lord is ever useless." (1 Corinthians 15:58/NLT)

STUDY QUESTIONS

1. Do you have children or younger siblings? If so, how have you purposefully mentored and trained them? If not, where have you looked for opportunities to mentor others?

2. Can you share an example of how mentoring someone else has impacted you?

3. What are some of the challenges that you have faced as a mentor? How were you able to overcome those challenges?

4. What are some aspects of Jesus' ministry that might help improve your mentoring skills?

5. Why do you think mentoring is an important element in today's society?

6. What are some specific ways that having more mentors might improve our nation?

7. What are some things you can do today that will help you embrace being a mentor (if you haven't already) or improving commitment to mentoring others?

FOLLOW THROUGH

• Find someone to mentor, and commit to meeting with them at least once a month.

• Read through and meditate on the scriptures found throughout this chapter. If you'd like to do some additional Bible study on being a mentor, here are some verses to get you started: Proverbs 9:9, Philippians 2:3-5, 1 Peter 5:2-3.

PRAYER

Lord, give me the desire to mentor someone else. Place people in my life who need whatever wisdom and knowledge I have to share. I want to be a part of the solution to the problems that our world is facing. Most importantly, I want those who I mentor to see Jesus in me. It's for Your glory. Amen.

CHAPTER THIRTEEN: CHRIST
FOLLOWING <u>THE</u> LEADER

"Follow my example, as I follow the example of Christ."
–1 Corinthians 11:1 (NIV)

Over the past twelve chapters, we've unpacked seven C's that are vitally important to anyone striving to become an effective leader. There are many other C's that we also could have discussed, such as care, certainty, clarity, collaboration, compassion, concentration, consideration, creativity, etc.

But none of the other C's will matter if you don't have the most important C active in your life: Christ—the foundational C that gives true meaning to all other leadership qualities.

SHAKY GROUND

In 2003, I was entering my fifth year as head coach at St. John's University. We had made three NCAA appearances (including the Elite Eight in 1999) and had just won the National Invitational Tournament (NIT) a few months earlier. I was promoting my first book, *Skills For Life*, co-written with Jonathan Peck, and a film in which I had a cameo (*The Perfect Score*) was soon to hit theaters.

Life was perfect—or so it seemed.

There's a detailed version of everything that happened next in the book, *Everybody Needs A Head Coach*. The abridged version goes something like this: a hot shot coach lands a major conference job in the Big Apple. Winning becomes more important than the love of the game and preparing players for life after basketball. Contentious contract negotiations combined with a rough start to the season turn into an unexpected termination.

Things get even worse after an NCAA investigation claims to have uncovered illegal payments to a former player. Although ultimately proven innocent of those unsubstantiated charges, the damage is done and the difficult process of self-reflection begins.

What's more important to understand is *why* everything started to fall apart. Unlike my wife, Connie, who had committed her life to Christ at a very young age, I had spent most of my adult life going through the motions. So many good things had happened to me throughout my career. I started to think that I was the primary reason for my success. I didn't realize that God had been the master puppeteer. He was the one pulling the strings that allowed me to be in that position.

But I didn't see that, because my foundation wasn't rooted in Christ. All along, I had been walking on shaky ground. Thank God, even when we mess up, there's a greater reason that we can't see until later.

A FIRM FOUNDATION

Connie and I knew we needed to get as far away from New York as possible. Again, the story of what happened next can be found in *Everybody Needs A Head Coach*, but the most important thing to know as it pertains to leadership is *who* changed everything for me.

His name was David Nicholas and he was the Senior Pastor at Spanish River Church in Boca Raton, Florida. I'm convinced that God led us to that church for the express purpose of introducing us to David who was totally committed to sharing the gospel with anyone he met. It didn't matter who you were or where you were. He was going to get around to sharing the bad news and the good news of Christ.

After a few months of building up a relationship, David made sure to ask me some tough questions. The first one was the toughest: "If you died tonight, where would you wake up? Would you be in Heaven with God, or would you be in Hell with the devil?"

I had always believed that I was a good person and good people go to Heaven, but David showed me that no one but Jesus is truly good:

For all have sinned and fall short of the glory of God. (Romans 3:23/NIV)

He then explained to me that because God is righteous and just, He couldn't accept me in my present condition. God had to hold me accountable for the sins I had committed against Him. David then recited Romans 6:23: *For the wages of sin is death, but the free gift of God is eternal life through Christ Jesus, our Lord.*

He made it perfectly clear that even if I only sinned one time, it would be enough to separate me from God. That was the bad news. Next came the good news.

David taught me how to repent of my sins. He showed me how to completely surrender my heart to Christ and make Him the Lord of my life. I prayed that prayer and made that commitment. To this day, I still celebrate April 29, 2005 as my second birthday—the day that I became a new creation in Christ.

Over the next five and a half years, David modeled what it looked like to be a spiritual leader. He showed me how important it was to have Christ as the foundation for everything I did as a coach, husband, father, brother, and public figure.

I would love to say that there was a 180-degree change in my life. Not true. Thankfully, however, my conversion allowed me to see my flaws with greater clarity. With the Holy Spirit's help, I was able to correct things that didn't reflect Christ.

Three years later I took the head coaching position at Florida Atlantic University. Winning was still important to me, but it was by no means the most important part of my job description. Unlike the past, I now understood that my primary responsibility was to expose my players to what it means to have a relationship with Christ. Prayer was an important part of what we did, and the Bible was an integral part of my teaching.

At the end of the day, nobody really cares about your achievements anyway. When you're gone, they're going to remember the kind of person you were. They're going to remember how much you cared about them. They're going to remember that you loved God and loved people. That's how I will always remember Pastor Nicholas.

David went to be with Jesus in January of 2011, but the legacy he left behind as a Christian leader is still being felt today and will continue for years to come. My life is one of the countless many that was changed for eternity.

UPON THIS ROCK

Two of the greatest leaders in church history were two of the least likely people to take up such a hefty mantle. In other words, they were flawed men who made plenty of mistakes along the way.

First, there was a fisherman named Simon. He was an average fisherman who, to the natural eye at least, was seemingly at the right place at the right time. In Luke 5:5-11, we read about one day when Jesus was teaching a group of people that had gathered near the lakeshore. Simon was cleaning his nets when Jesus asked if He could borrow his boat. Simon obliged, and Jesus sat in the boat while he continued to teach the crowd.

When Jesus was finished speaking, he told Simon to take the boat out into the deep water and let his nets down to catch some fish. Simon scoffed at the idea. He hadn't caught anything all day. Still, understanding that there was something different about Jesus, he went ahead and did as He asked.

Simon dropped his nets, and when he pulled them back up, they were so full they began to break. His partners came over to help secure the miraculous bounty. For Simon, it was the first real revelation that Jesus was no ordinary man. So when Jesus asked Simon to follow Him, it wasn't a very hard decision to make.

That didn't mean things always went well. Simon's flaws showed up at various stages of his relationship with Jesus. He was tempestuous. He was unruly. He was rough around the edges. But, he was also passionate. He was inquisitive. He was fiercely loyal.

And yes, he made plenty of mistakes. Still, Jesus had big plans for Simon and prophesied his destiny when He gave him the name by which he is now famously known: *"Now I say to you that you are Peter (which means 'rock'), and upon this rock I will build my church, and all the powers of hell will not conquer it." (Matthew 16:18/NLT)*

After Jesus' death, resurrection, and ascension back to Heaven, Peter became a strong, bold leader whose mission was to spread the gospel all over the known world—a far cry from the flawed fisherman who encountered the Messiah on that fateful day.

STRUCK DOWN

As Peter was leading the newly formed church, another man was seeking to destroy it. His name was Saul, and his story provides a fascinating character study on misguided leadership. Saul looked good on paper, but that meant nothing because he was following the wrong leader—himself. He was arrogant and held tightly to a sense of entitlement.

Saul was unique because he was Jewish *and* had Roman citizenship. He was an influential zealot who was willing to do whatever it took to preserve his religious way of life. Saul hunted down converted Jews and persecuted them through imprisonment, torture, and sometimes death. That was his mission.

I can relate to Saul. He had a lot of pride and had the wrong motivations. He had created his own kingdom and would do whatever it took to protect it. I can also relate to what happened next in Saul's story (found in Acts 9).

While traveling to the town called Damascus, Saul was blinded by a bright light and brought to his knees.

"Saul! Saul! Why are you persecuting me?"

"Who are you, Lord?" Saul asked.

And the voice replied, "I am Jesus, the one you are persecuting! Now get up and go into the city, and you will be told what you must do." (vv. 4-6)

When Saul got up, he opened his eyes but could not see. His traveling companions took him to Damascus where he remained blind for three days and refused to eat or drink until Saul's sight was eventually restored. From that moment, his new life as a minster of the gospel began. His transformation was nothing less than miraculous. Saul changed his name to Paul and is today known as the greatest evangelist the church as ever known. Paul's letters to the early Christians make up a large portion of the New Testament, and his spirit-led insights are still impacting millions of people today.

It usually takes an awakening to get us back on the right path. For me, it was getting fired. For Paul, it was a harsh wakeup call in the form of a vision from Jesus. It may not always be fun to go through, but God will use those things—sometimes very bad things—to create that change in our lives. I was stripped of the fame and the glory, but just like Paul, God had a bigger purpose for me, and now He has me exactly where He wants me.

SEVEN KEYS TO FOLLOWING THE LEADER: CHRIST

The more I learned about Peter and Paul and other biblical heroes such as Abraham, Moses, and David, I realized that if God could use those flawed men, he could use me. We all can relate to them in one way or another because we are all imperfect.

That's why we all need to be reminded from time to time that doing things in our strength will never work out. We can never truly fulfill the promise of our God-ordained destiny until our foundation is Christ—nothing more, nothing less.

If you want to reach your full potential and become the leader that He has called you to be, here are seven keys to following <u>the</u> leader—Jesus Christ:

1. Let Him Change Your Heart. Our motives aren't always as pure as we'd like to think. Human nature can subtly creep in and turn even the best intentions into self-driven action. Ask Jesus to root out any hidden sin and replace it with the fruits of the Spirit.

"Therefore, if anyone is in Christ, the new creation has come: The old has gone, the new is here!" (2 Corinthians 5:17/NIV)

2. Submit To His Authority. There's no true success in life if you're not following Jesus. Make Him Lord of your life, and give Him your allegiance and trust.

"Then Jesus came to them and said, 'All authority in heaven and on earth has been given to me.'" (Matthew 28:18/NIV)

3. Study His Ways. Jesus is the greatest leader to walk this earth. There's no better path to great leadership apart from studying the way that He led the disciples.

"If you hold to my teaching, you are really my disciples. Then you will know the truth, and the truth will set you free." (John 8:31b-32/NIV)

4. Fellowship With The Leader. Talk to Jesus. Listen to Him. Work on having a daily relationship with Him. That, along with studying His Word, will help you truly know Him.

"I am the vine; you are the branches. If you remain in me and I in you, you will bear much fruit; apart from me you can do nothing. If you do not remain in me, you are like a branch that is thrown away and withers; such branches are picked up, thrown into the fire and burned. If you remain in me and my words remain in you, ask whatever you wish, and it will be done for you. This is to my Father's glory, that you bear much fruit, showing yourselves to be my disciples." (John 15:5-8/NIV)

5. Trust His Plan. Have faith in Jesus. Trust that He will lead you down the right path and in the right direction. Jesus always has your best interests in mind.

"The LORD will guide you always; he will satisfy your needs in a sun-scorched land and will strengthen your frame. You will be like a well-watered garden, like a spring whose waters never fail." (Isaiah 58:11/NIV)

6. Practice What He Preached. It's an ongoing process, but you have to work at being more like Jesus. It's a daily thing that requires patience, perseverance, and consistency.

"Whoever claims to live in him must live as Jesus did." (1 John 2:6/NIV)

7. Stand Up For Truth. Following Jesus means resisting the temptation to be politically correct. Once you choose that path, you must do the right thing no matter the cost. You instantly become a target when you stand for truth. It's not easy, but stand firm. Compromise is not an option.

"You will be hated by everyone because of me, but the one who stands firm to the end will be saved." (Matthew 10:22/NIV)

STUDY QUESTIONS

1. Can you describe a time in your life when you felt like you were on shaky ground?

2. Can you describe a time in your life when you felt like you were standing on solid ground? What was the difference between the two instances?

3. What are some aspects of the stories from this chapter (Coach Jarvis, Peter, and Paul) to which you can relate?

4. What are some of Jesus' characteristics that, in your opinion, make Him such a dynamic leader?

5. On a scale of one to ten, what is your current Commitment level to Jesus as your leader (one = not committed at all, ten = 100% committed)? What factors would you say are having the biggest impact (positive or negative) on your Commitment to Jesus?

6. Of the seven keys listed, which ones are you struggling with the most? Explain.

7. What are some things that you can start doing today that will help you have a stronger Commitment to Jesus as your leader?

FOLLOW THROUGH

• Write out your testimony. Explain what you were like before you were saved, when you accepted Jesus as your Lord and Savior, and how that changed your life. You can find mine, "Meet My Head Coach," at www.coachmikejarvis.com.

• Share your testimony whenever the opportunity presents itself.

• Engage in daily devotionals. If you like, you can start with my twenty-three-day devotional, "Everybody Needs A Head Coach," which can be found at www.coachmikejarvis.com.

• Commit John 3:16 to memory:

"For God so loved the world that He gave His only begotten Son, that whoever believes in Him shall not perish, but have eternal life."

Then, ask the Lord to help you bring others to salvation as the Holy Spirit leads.

• Read through and meditate on the scriptures found throughout this chapter. If you'd like to do some additional Bible study on Christ, here are some verses to get you started: 1 Corinthians 11:1, 2 Corinthians 5:17, 1 John 2:6.

PRAYER

Lord, I acknowledge that nothing I ever do as a leader will matter if I'm not following Jesus. Give me a greater passion to study His words, understand His heart, fellowship with Him, and submit to His authority. Help me be more like Him every day. Amen.

If you have yet to accept Jesus as Your Lord and Savior and want to do so now, read and sincerely believe this prayer with all of your heart:

Lord Jesus, I come to you, acknowledging that I am a sinner and cannot make myself acceptable to You through my own efforts. I believe You went to the Cross as my substitute, to be judged in my place, and by doing so You saved me from the judgment I deserve. You did for me what I could not do for myself. I trust You to give me a new life that works, and I know You are the only One who can give it to me. Furthermore, I believe with all of my heart and soul that You are the way, the truth, and the life, and that no one can come to the Father except through You. Lord Jesus, please give me the necessary strength and wisdom to live like You so that I may successfully complete the work You sent me here to do. Amen.

BONUS CHAPTER: CASH
STEWARDING YOUR RESOURCES

"The trustworthy person will get a rich reward, but a person who wants quick riches will get into trouble."
–Proverbs 28:20 (NLT)

If I could get a few mulligans for certain parts of my life, there are certainly a lot of things I would do differently. At the top of the list would be how I handled my finances.

You think you're going to work and make good money for a long time, but if you're not careful, it's easy to get complacent and not take care of that money or make plans for your long-term future.

That's why we have included a bonus chapter at the end of this book to talk about the biblical principles of Cash that all leaders should understand and hopefully put into practice. It's never too late to learn how to be a better steward of your resources in the home, in the workplace, in the church, or in the Community at large.

LIVE TO GIVE

When Connie and I moved to Boca Raton, Florida, we slowed down long enough to start thinking more seriously about our financial future. Through that process, we met Pete Striano who is a managing partner at Northwestern Mutual. Pete didn't just help me put together a sensible plan, but he also became a dear friend to my family and me.

Pete had a significant impact on my son, Mike, who was so impressed with Pete that he joined the Northwestern family when he transitioned out of the coaching profession and had the benefit of Pete's leadership and mentoring.

Over time, I learned a lot about Pete's life and what motivated him to serve his clients and, more importantly, serve his family and the Community. Pete was raised in a traditional, Italian family. His father worked a variety of jobs, which allowed his mom to raise the kids and take care of the home. Pete's dad was a sheet metal worker, a special education teacher, and an employee at the Turkey Point nuclear facility in Homestead, Florida. He also became very successful in the real estate finance business.

Pete's dad taught him about hard work, Commitment, integrity, and legacy. Then, Pete went to college at Florida Atlantic University and capitalized on an opportunity to intern at Northwestern Mutual. After graduating, he got a job there and quickly moved up the ranks.

Long before his professional career, however, Pete had learned something else from his dad: "No one goes through life undefeated."

In other words, there will always be people around you who are going through tough times and need some help. That became a reality that Pete would focus on at the workplace. At an office holiday party, for instance, he and his colleagues learned about a young girl battling a life threatening brain tumor. Her family had insurance, but it didn't cover everything, including travel costs to Boston for treatment.

"We were at a nice restaurant enjoying ourselves," Pete recalls. "But helping that girl was much more important than having a good time. We wanted to do something with the night that had a greater purpose, so we raised $5,000 for the girl and her family."

Pete also led the charge when Our Father's House soup kitchen in Pompano, Florida, was struggling to keep its doors open. The volunteer-based organization didn't have an adequate fence, weren't able to maintain building codes, and the city was exploring development opportunities that would make the soup kitchen expendable.

"That ministry was a life line for thousands of people in that Community," Pete explains. "So Northwestern donated money for a new fence, helped get the building up to code, provided new signage, and covered some of the meal costs to make sure no one went hungry."

In 2012, as a continuation of its mission to impact the Community, Northwestern Mutual set a goal of raising funds to help eradicate and cure pediatric cancer. Through financial donations, the company has given millions of dollars toward that effort.

"You can't leave the earth with your material wealth," Pete says. "You can't put it in your coffin when you die. When you are successful, God will judge you on what you do with that success. To whom much is given, much is required. What are you going to do with it to help other people?"

Northwestern Mutual is also impacting positive change through its financial literacy programs for kids. The company has developed a website called www.themint.com, which teaches young people how to better understand their lifelong relationship with money and why it's so important to be a good steward of their material resources.

One of their more effective tools is a piggy bank that divides money into four key areas:

1. Money you need to spend.
2. Money you need to save.
3. Money you need to invest.
4. Money you need to give.

That last item on the list is ultimately the most important. Pete's personal mission is to help the next generation understand why their most significant calling in life is to "live to give." From there, the sky is the limit on what God can do next through those who accept the challenge to be His hands and feet.

"When you give, you can impact at least one life," Pete says. "And if you impact at least one life, you've changed the world."

LITTLE IS MUCH

Jesus had a lot to say about money and material wealth. Here are just a few key points from His teachings on Cash:

• Don't get too comfortable with material wealth. (Matthew 6:19-21)

• Don't put material things before God. (Matthew 6:24)

• Put God first, and your material needs will be met. (Matthew 6:33)

• Give generously. (Matthew 5:42)

• Fulfill your financial obligations—even taxes. (Mark 12:14-17)

• God requires us to be good stewards of our resources. (Matthew 25:14-30)

One of His most powerful statements about money, however, was a brief but meaningful illustration He shared with His disciples in the temple. While there, they observed the wealthy people putting substantial amounts of money into the treasury. For the average onlooker, it was certainly an impressive display. It was someone else, however, that caught Jesus' attention:

He saw also a certain poor widow putting in two mites (a penny). So He said, "Truly I say to you that this poor widow has put in more than all; for all these out of their abundance have put in offerings for God, but she out of her poverty put in all the livelihood that she had." (Luke 21:1-4/NKJV)

Jesus taught three valuable lessons in that very short passage:

1) It isn't the amount of money given that matters, but rather it's the heart *behind* the giving that God cares about the most.

2) Sacrificial giving carries more weight in God's economy.

3) Little is much when your giving is directed toward the Kingdom of God.

Each of those three points are tied to even greater biblical principles. First of all, every financial decision we make is based on either what we want for ourselves or what God wants for us. It's a heart issue that needs to be addressed. Are we consistently giving into our <u>pride</u> and serving our own needs, or are we thinking first about what God wants or requires in any given situation?

Secondly, stewardship (or the lack thereof) is often an issue of <u>trust</u>. When we hold our money with clenched hands, it's telling God that we don't trust Him with our finances. When we give freely and generously, however, we are telling God that we are fully confident in His ability to take care of our needs no matter what the accounting ledger might say.

Finally, the way we steward our money either shows great <u>faith</u> or a lack of belief that God can do great things with our financial offerings, especially the ones that are small. Jesus showed us through His ministry what He is capable of doing with little. There is no greater example than when He took fives loaves of bread and two small fish from a young boy and multiplied it for more than five thousand people. (John 6:1-15)

That's the question we should all ponder. Where do pride, trust, and faith fit into our financial narratives? An honest answer to each of those three areas will either reveal a steward worthy of God's blessing or a person who will struggle with money throughout their lifetime.

SEVEN KEYS TO STEWARDING YOUR RESOURCES

Stewardship is a biblical principle that God clearly cares about. How we manage our resources reveals the inner desires of our hearts, and when we manage our resources well, it allows us to be more effective as providers for our family and overseers of our businesses finances, and gives us the freedom to give with a spirit of abundance.

With that goal in mind, here are seven keys that will help you become a better steward of your resources:

1. Envision Your Future. You can't get to where you want to be if you don't know where you want to go. It's important to chart your course and write down exactly what you want your financial future to look like.

> "This vision is for a future time.
> It describes the end, and it will be fulfilled.
> If it seems slow in coming, wait patiently,
> for it will surely take place.
> It will not be delayed." (Habbakuk 2:3/NLT)

2. Assess Your Assets. Sometimes it's easy to get discouraged, thinking about what you don't have. Try something different. Think about what you *do* have, which is more than you may realize. Take a personal inventory of your skills (non-monetary resources) and create a balance sheet of your life (adding in your current income and other monetary assets). This will give you a better understand of how much you need to spend, how much you need to save, and what it will take to reach your goals.

"In his grace, God has given us different gifts for doing certain things well." (Romans 12:6a/NLT)

3. Make A Budget. Many American families spend more time planning a summer vacation than on their annual budget. The lack of financial foresight has contributed to a cascading fiscal crisis throughout our communities. Not having a budget will assuredly lead to debt and a host of problems that are not easily overcome.

"Suppose one of you wants to build a tower. Won't you first sit down and estimate the cost to see if you have enough money to complete it?" (Luke 14:28/NIV)

4. Chip Away At Your Debt. In today's economic culture, it sometimes seems impossible to avoid getting into some level of debt. Credit cards, home mortgages, and car payments are just a few ways we can find ourselves in fiscal trouble. Don't stay there! Work with a financial advisor or put together your own plan and make sure that your debt doesn't do serious harm to your future. If you stick with it, the debt cycle will turn into savings, investment, and giving.

"The wicked borrow and never repay, but the godly are generous givers." (Psalm 37:21/NLT)

5. Save As You Go. It can be difficult to put money aside when you're living paycheck to paycheck or trying to get out of debt. Saving money, however, is a valuable discipline that will literally pay off in the long term.

"Wealth gained hastily will dwindle, but whoever gathers little by little will increase it." (Proverbs 13:11/ESV)

6. Get Insured. In Old Testament times, there wasn't insurance as we know it today, but God instructed His people on how to have a backup plan for tough times. Joseph used this principle to save Egypt, (Genesis 41) and we too can rely on modern amenities such as life insurance, health insurance, home insurance, disability insurance, and long-term care insurance to protect us from financial ruin and protect our family's financial security.

"A prudent person foresees danger and takes precautions. The simpleton goes blindly on and suffers the consequences." (Proverbs 27:12/NLT)

7. Give It Away. There are three primary reasons that we should aspire to financial prosperity: to take care of our family, to invest in the Kingdom of God, and to bless others. Whether it's through tithing (Malachi 3:10) or charitable donations (Acts 20:35), giving your money away is an act of obedience and a sign that you are trusting God to be your ultimate source.

"Remember this: Whoever sows sparingly will also reap sparingly, and whoever sows generously will also reap generously. Each of you should give what you have decided in your heart to give, not reluctantly or under compulsion, for God loves a cheerful giver." (2 Corinthians 9:6-7/NIV)

STUDY QUESTIONS

1. How would you describe your current relationship with money?

2. In what areas do you struggle to be a good steward? In what areas have you done a good job?

3. On scale of one to ten (one not significant at all, ten being most significant), what level of importance do you place on giving of your resources to others? Explain.

4. Of Jesus' teachings on money that are mentioned, which would you say are operating in your life? With which of those teachings do you struggle? Explain.

5. Go through each of the following areas (pride, trust, and faith) and discuss how they impact your financial decisions?

6. Go back and look over the seven keys to stewarding your resources. Which ones are you currently following? Which ones are you not following and why? How has not following those keys impacted your finances?

7. What are some steps that you can take today that will make you a better steward of your financial resources? How do you think taking those steps will change your life?

FOLLOW THROUGH

- Make a list of your resources.

- Create a personal budget. Make sure to include areas for personal needs, giving, saving, and investing.

- Complete the "Input of Influences" and "Gratitude Assessment" (Appendix B).

- Read through and meditate on the scriptures found throughout this chapter. If you'd like to do some additional Bible study on Cash, here are some verses to get you started: Here are a few to get you started: Psalm 37:21, Proverbs 28:20, 2 Corinthians 9:6-7.

PRAYER

Lord, give me a vision for my material resources. Help me do a better job managing my money so that I might be blessed to be a blessing. Root out any covetous attitudes in my heart. Everything I have is Yours. I put you in charge of my storehouse and trust that You will help me make financial decisions that honor You and build up Your Kingdom. Amen.

APPENDIX A
PERSONAL LEADERSHIP INVENTORY

On the following pages, you will find a set of questions that correspond to each chapter of the book. We believe that this is an exercise for everyone—young or old, seasoned or not. Your honest answer to each question will give you a good idea of the areas in which you, or the person you are helping/mentoring, could stand some improvement.

A careful analysis of the inventory results will identify those areas in which the greatest work and improvement is needed. We recommend that you retake the inventory when you have completed the book and its discussion guides.

We hope that the Personal Leadership Inventory will encourage you to develop an individual approach to *The Seven C's of Leadership*. There is no one prescribed way to make the most of the information this provides. It has been specifically organized to be used either as a reference for specific areas, or as a comprehensive curriculum for self-improvement.

The Seven C's of Leadership has been a passion of ours for a number of years. We hope that our passion comes through in the book and that our readers enjoy using it as a road map for their own life journeys.

• •

Grading Scale:
0 = Never
1 = Once in a while
2 = Half of the time
3 = Most of the time
4 = Always

CONFIDENCE
• A parent/mentor has helped me develop my Confidence. ____

• I look for opportunities to show my abilities. ____

• I seek out experiences that will extend my knowledge. ____

• I make an effort to share my experiences with others.   _____

• Confidence is a life skill that can be learned.   _____

• I remain Confident during tough times.

_____

TOTAL: _____

COURAGE
• It is not difficult for me to make a decision when I disagree with
with the majority's opinion.   _____

• If there is a possibility I may not succeed, I will try anyway.   _____

• If I had an opportunity to improve my future, I would sacrifice my
present lifestyle.   _____

• God has a plan for my life.   _____

• I stand for truth rather than popular opinion.   _____

TOTAL: _____

CHARACTER I
• I would describe myself as a person of good Character.   _____

• Character is something you can develop or attain.   _____

• Character includes the ability to stand by your beliefs and convictions. _____

• I have people of good Character in my life.   _____

• I try to associate with people of Character.   _____

TOTAL   _____

CHARACTER II
• I ask for God's will in all my decisions.   _____

• I recognize that negative emotions (anger, jealousy, fear, doubt, guilt,
sadness, etc.) can cause poor judgment when unchecked.   _____

• I look at situations carefully, and patiently pursue solutions. _____

• I seek wise counsel when making major decisions. _____

TOTAL _____

COMMITMENT

• When things are not going the way I expect, I stay Committed to the cause.

_____

• I will remain Committed even if the situation is unpopular. _____

• I am Committed to other people and their needs. _____

• I keep my Commitments. _____

TOTAL _____

COMMUNICATION I

• I observe and listen before I speak. _____

• I ask good questions. _____

• I listen with an open mind. _____

• I focus on the positive. _____

• I encourage others to contribute to share their thoughts. _____

• I choose my words carefully and think before I speak. _____

TOTAL _____

COMMUNICATION II

• I know how to pay attention. _____

• I try to make a good first impression. _____

• I am willing and able to share a core message of my faith when the opportunity presents itself. _____

• I present my message in a way that will make people want to know more.

_____

• I listen with my eyes and my ears.   _____

TOTAL   _____

COMMUNITY I
• Family is very important to me.   _____

• I believe that marriage is a lifelong Commitment.   _____

• I put God in the center of my marriage.   _____

• I seek wise counsel for advice on family matters.   _____

• I actively try to learn more about being a better spouse/parent.   _____

• I communicate regularly with my spouse/children to talk about the vision
and purpose for our family.   _____

TOTAL   _____

COMMUNITY II

• I lead by example.   _____

• I create written and verbal guidelines for others to follow. _____

• I will give a second chance to someone who has messed up.   _____

• I will apologize when I am wrong.   _____

TOTAL   _____

COMMUNITY III
• I am motivated to do things by compassion.   _____

• I am actively involved in my Community.   _____

• I try to associate with like-minded people.   _____

• Serving others is part of my DNA.   _____

TOTAL   _____

COACH I
- I know when I need someone to mentor me. ____

- I am willing to accept constructive criticism. ____

- I am open and honest with my mentor. ____

- I recognize my strengths and weaknesses. ____

- I appreciate the time and effort that my mentor has invested in me. ____

TOTAL ____

COACH II
- I enjoy investing my time, talents, and treasures to help others reach their full potential. ____

- Before advising others, I do my research to gather as much information as possible. ____

- I love serving others. ____

- I try to ask thought-provoking questions. ____

- I realize that mentoring is a two-way street. ____

TOTAL ____

CASH
- My faith plays a role in how I view money. ____

- I make a budget and stick to it. ____

- I have a plan for financial savings. ____

- Me and my family's health and material assets are insured. ____

- I give to my church, community, etc. ____

TOTAL ____

APPENDIX B
INPUT OF INFLUENCES & GRATITUDE ASSESSMENT

INPUT OF INFLUENCES

Assessing Your Input

Let's look at all the potential ways you are feeding your mind. Just put a zero if you don't do a particular activity.

ACTIVITY	TIME		
	Per Day	**Per Week**	**Total Per Year**
Read Bible			
Spend time in prayer			
Morning TV			
Radio in the car			
Evening TV			
Games on cell phone			
Online gaming			
Facebook			
Snapchat			
Gossip blogs			
Gossip magazines			
Surfing on the web			
Instagram			
YouTube			

List three ways you will cut or significantly limit your input of negative information, fear mongering, gossip, and worrisome or needless social commentary.

1. _____

_____

2. _____

_____

3. _____

Your Plan to Feed Your Mind

List three ways you will be proactive in positively feeding your mind.

1. _____

_____

2. _____

_____

3. _____

_____

GRATITUDE ASSESSEMENT

Three amazing people in my life are:

1. _____

_____

2. _____

_____

3. _____

_____

Three great things about my physical body are:

1. _____

_____

2. _____

_____

3. _____

_____

Three great things about my home and where I live are:

1. _____

_____

2. _____

_____

3. _____

_____

Three great things about where I work or go to school are:

1. _____

_____

2. _____

_____

3. _____

_____

Three skills or unique talents I have been given are:

1. _____

_____

2. _____

_____

3. _____

_____

Three ways I have been blessed in my life are:

1. _____

_____

2. _____

_____

3. _____

_____

Three ways in which my life is prosperous are:

1. _____

   _____

2. _____

   _____

3. _____

   _____

ABOUT THE AUTHORS

MIKE JARVIS is a legendary basketball coach, author, and inspirational speaker. In his first head coaching job, he led Cambridge Rindge and Latin High School and future Hall of Famer, Patrick Ewing, to three consecutive state championships with a record of 77-1. In twenty-five years as a Division I men's basketball coach, Coach Jarvis guided Boston University, George Washington, St. John's, and Florida Atlantic to fourteen postseason appearances that included trips to the Sweet Sixteen and the Elite Eight. In 1997, he was elected President of the National Association of Basketball Coaches. A year later, he was named National Coach of the Year by the Black Coaches Association and Father of the Year by *Ebony Magazine.* Coach Jarvis ended his high school and collegiate coaching career with an overall head coaching record of 684–351. He has written three books including, *Skills for Life* and *Everybody Needs a Head Coach*, and currently serves as an Adjunct Professor at the South Florida Bible College and Theological Seminary where he teaches Leadership Skills. Coach Jarvis and his wife, Connie, have a son, Mike II, a daughter, Dana, five grandchildren, and reside in Boynton Beach, Florida.

CHAD BONHAM is a mass media veteran with 30 years of extensive experience as an author, journalist, marketing consultant, and film producer. He has written for over thirty national publications and has authored, co-authored, or ghost written twenty-six books including, *Faith in the Fast Lane* (Judson Press), *Life in the Fairway* (New Leaf), *3D Coach* (Regal Books), and *Everybody Needs A Head Coach* (Cross Training Publishing). Chad resides in Broken Arrow, Okla., with his wife, Amy, and their three sons, Lance, Cole, and Quinn.

INDEX